CITYSPOTS
SOFIA

Sean Sheehan

G000272386

Written by Sean Sheehan
Original photography by Sean Sheehan
Front cover photography © Russell Young/www.photolibrary.com
Series design based on an original concept by Studio 183 Limited

Produced by Cambridge Publishing Management Limited
Project Editor: Karen Beaulah
Layout: Paul Queripel
Maps: PC Graphics
Transport map: © Communicarta Limited

Published by Thomas Cook Publishing
A division of Thomas Cook Tour Operations Limited
Company Registration No. 1450464 England
PO Box 227, Unit 18, Coningsby Road
Peterborough PE3 8SB, United Kingdom
email: books@thomascook.com
www.thomascookpublishing.com
+ 44 (0) 1733 416477

ISBN-13: 978-184157-728-9
ISBN-10: 1-84157-728-6

First edition © 2006 Thomas Cook Publishing
Text © 2006 Thomas Cook Publishing
Maps © 2006 Thomas Cook Publishing
Series Editor: Kelly Anne Pipes
Project Editor: Ross Hilton
Production/DTP: Steven Collins

Printed and bound in Spain by GraphyCems

CONTENTS

SYMBOLS & ABBREVIATIONS

The following symbols are used throughout this book:

a address   **t** telephone   **f** fax   **e** email   **w** website address
L opening times   **N** public transport connections   **i** important

The following symbols are used on the maps:

i information office   O city
✈ airport   O large town
+ hospital   ○ small town
◉ police station   ═ motorway
▣ bus station   ▬ main road
◢ railway station   ▭ minor road
M metro   ▬ railway
† cathedral
① numbers denote featured cafés & restaurants

Hotels and restaurants are graded by approximate price as follows:
£ budget   **££** mid-range   **£££** expensive

O *The multi-domed Alexander Nevsky Memorial Church*

INTRODUCING
Sofia

Introduction

Europe's youngest capital – only established as such in 1879 – has all the attractiveness of precocious youth: unsophisticated, vigorously alive, relishing an undiluted urge for fun and late hours. Remarkably inexpensive bars, cafés, restaurants, pubs and piano bars are everywhere and closing times for all such places are commonly 02.00, seven days a week. Less than a decade ago, no one could have imagined that staid and stodgy Sofia would morph into an epicurean outpost in the bleak Balkans. The metamorphosis is ongoing, and when you settle into a café-restaurant-bar – Sofia's secular trinity – you too become part of the process and start to soak up the unique character of this most surprising of European capitals.

Sofia is compact, and the hotels, restaurants and bars that will compete for your time are nearly all located within a tidily arranged city centre that is minutes from the airport. The city has a distinct European flavour with its broad boulevards and countless number of open-air watering holes, but there are intriguing reminders of its more Eastern heritage in the form of Byzantine- and Russian-inspired churches. The most immediate, and daily, reminder that that you are deep inside Eastern Europe comes when you grapple with street and place names that use the Cyrillic alphabet. It is part of the fun of being somewhere different, and you cannot get seriously lost because the city centre is too small. Trams and astonishingly cheap taxis will take you anywhere that is not within walking distance.

What may at first seem a deficit of conventional attractions turns out to be a refreshing lack of manufactured tourism. There are museums and galleries to visit, but not so many as to exhaust yourself tramping from one must-see sight to another. Two or three days will easily cover the ground, and if your stay is any longer then it is time to take an excursion. There are two neighbouring towns with very contrasting characters, and the ski slopes at Mount Vitosha are a convenient six-minute bus ride away from one of the city's bus terminals.

◬ *Sofia is a young person's city*

When to go

SEASONS & CLIMATE

Sofia's climate is continental, and while the summers are hot and sunny, the winter months can be very cold. January is the coldest, with the mercury dipping below zero at night, and the months either side are not noticeably different. This is certainly not a problem if skiing is on your agenda and you are above 800 m (2,625 ft) to enjoy blue skies and crisp snow, wearing the right clothing. On sunny days, the daytime temperature can be 20°C (68°F) in the sun, though well below zero at night. Come March, temperatures start rising to around 5°C (41°F) and continue to rise by 10° each month for the next three months. April to June is a lovely time to be in Sofia, with alfresco eating and drinking being

„Време за полет.“

● *'Time for flight' – hurtling through the crisp mountain air* the order of the day; the weather is ideal for excursions into the countryside and airfares have not peaked. The public parks become attractions in their own right and are ideal for long picnics. In June the temperature is 19°C (66°F) and stays in the mid-20s°C (70s°F) throughout July and August, the hottest months of the year, until dropping back to June's average in September. Temperatures then plummet by 10° each month, and by the end of November the first snow has fallen above 1,000 m (3,281 ft). December brings the freezing cold once more, and throughout the winter months Sofia is usually covered by a grey and heavy smog, making this period the least attractive time to make a visit (especially when fog causes flight delays at the airport).

ANNUAL EVENTS
January–March
The main months of the **skiing season**, although usually lasting until well into April.

February
Religious holiday 2 February is celebrated as the 40th day since the birth of Christ, and solemn evening services take place in all the churches. Baptised youngsters are brought to the service by their mothers.

March
International Women's Day This is celebrated in Sofia on 8 March with female employees being taken out to lunch.
Sofia's international film festival The first half of March brings this festival, now over ten years old and still going strong. ❶ (02) 916 6029 Ⓦ www.cinema.bg/sff

April

Easter This brings dedicated services in the churches, and special concerts often take place around this time.

April–May

Drama Festival Stretching over late April and early May, a drama festival takes place in Blagoevgrad.

May–June

Festival of classical music and ballet Usually at the end of May and lasting well into June, the National Palace of Culture (NDK) is the main venue for the larger concerts and performances. Tickets can be

---

PUBLIC HOLIDAYS

Banks, post offices, government offices and many shops and businesses are closed on public holidays, but restaurants and bars are not affected and public transport runs according to the usual schedules.

New Year's Day 1 Jan
Signing of the San Stefano treaty in 1878 which secured Bulgaria's independence from Turkish rule 3 Mar
Easter Sun and Mon Apr
Labour Day 1 May
Day of the Cyrillic alphabet, celebrating the brothers Cyril and Methodius, founders of the Bulgarian alphabet 24 May
Unification Day 6 Sept
Independence Day 22 Sept
Christmas Day 25 Dec
New Year's Eve 31 Dec

bought in advance at the NDK ticket office (❶ (02) 916 6830
Ⓦ www.ndk.bg). Another venue is Zala Bulgaria (Bulgaria Hall),
home of the Bulgarian Philharmonic. ❸ Aksakov Street
❶ (02) 987 7656

August
The birthday of St John of Rila Rila Monastery is the venue for
special church services on 18 August.
Regional folk music festival Over the weekend closest to 15 August,
a regional folk music festival takes place in the small town of
Koprivshtitsa.

November
International Jazz Festival This takes place in Sofia in the second
week of the month.

Mid-December
There is usually enough snow on Mount Vitosha to kick-start the
skiing season.

MARCH & MARTINITSAS
At the start of March it is time to present friends and relatives
with *martinitsas* – entwined red and white woollen threads –
to bring them happiness and health. Sold everywhere, they are
worn on clothing or tied around the wrist until, so the
tradition goes, the first stork is seen. Sofia is not exactly
overcrowded with storks, but by the end of the month people
follow the custom of tying their *martinitsas* on to a fruit tree
in a park or garden.

On the brink

Soon, very soon, Sofia will become the capital of a new, fully fledged member of the European Union (EU), and the long wait will be finally over. In 2005, the Accession Treaty was signed and 2007 was set as year zero for full membership. Then, out of the blue for many people, came a report from the EU saying that the country had not made the economic and legal progress that had been expected and membership might have to be postponed until 2008. The problems – organised crime, corruption, a weak legal system and a damaged environment – are old ones that have plagued the country since the early 1990s when the old order collapsed in Eastern Europe. For the visitor, such problems are not discernible and Sofia seems very much a European city waiting to take its rightful place in the EU. When you take an excursion out of the city to Blagoevgrad or Koprivshtitsa, however, the journey by road opens up other views, and the despoiled countryside reveals a history of deprivation that desperately requires a massive injection of EU funds.

Back in Sofia, impatience becomes more palpable as the light at the end of the EU tunnel beckons. The city's new mayor is regarded as a dynamic and charismatic figure who will show the rest of the country what an EU city should look like. He promises to deal with traffic problems – though most visitors will find the scale of such problems laughably small – and tackle the potholes and the stray dogs that do indeed add a blemish to the surface of everyday life. In the meantime, enjoying the benefits of a stable economy and a steady growth rate of over 5 per cent, the young people of Sofia are dressing and partying like Euro-kids anywhere else on the continent. In their hearts they feel that good times have arrived and they are geared up to embrace it. Whether EU membership finally arrives in

2007 or 2008 is an issue for the politicians to sort out for they know with confidence they will still be young when the day does come – and they are ready.

🔺 *A reminder of the past – soldiers patrol outside the Presidential Palace*

History

Bulgaria was known as Thrace to the ancient Greeks and to the Romans who conquered the land and made possible its incorporation into the Byzantine Empire that was ruled from Constantinople (Istanbul). Slavs migrated into the region and mixed with the nomadic Bulgars, laying the basis for a Bulgarian kingdom that succumbed to the power of the Ottoman Empire in the late 14th century. It was half a millennium later, with the help of Russian support for Slav independence, that a war of liberation against Turkish rule finally proved effective and the Treaty of San Stefano in 1878 recognised a liberated Bulgaria.

Bulgaria fell to the Nazis in World War II but, heroically and almost uniquely, Bulgarian public opinion resisted Nazi demands and the willingness of their Nazi puppet government for the country's Jews to be transported to the death camps. After the war, the Bulgarian Communist Party emerged to take political control and the country became part of the Soviet bloc under the dictatorial rule of Todor Zhivkov. The Cold War period gave Bulgarians guaranteed work and free medical care, but the country's image suffered in the West. The secret police were blamed for the murder of dissident writer Georgi Markov, murdered on London's Waterloo Bridge in 1978 after being stabbed by a poison-tipped umbrella. Human rights campaigners drew attention to the persecution of racial minorities in Bulgaria itself. Sofia, none too surprisingly, was not a favourite holiday destination for Westerners.

The winds of change fanned by Gorbachev in Moscow swept into Bulgaria, and by the late 1980s economic and political life was beginning to change radically. As elsewhere in Eastern Europe, events moved swiftly and dramatically. On 10 November 1989, the day after the Berlin Wall came down, a power struggle and ideological split within the ruling party led to the removal of the old order – Zhivkov exited stage left – and the promise of free elections and a multiparty system. A new government emerged after elections in 1991, and the old system was dismantled. However, the unleashing of an untamed capitalism led to widespread inequities as the gap between rich and poor widened obscenely and polarised the country. By 1996, hyper-inflation was reaching nearly 600 per cent and crippling the country. Street protests and strikes in 1997 led to a new caretaker government under the popular mayor of Sofia, and relative stability emerged from the chaos. The social divisions, nonetheless, remained, and these help to explain the strange events of 2001. Simeon Saxe-Coburg Gotha, Tsar in exile since he was expelled by the Communists after World War II, returned to the country only two months before parliamentary elections. He formed a new party, promising to stamp out corruption, and he won with a landslide victory.

By 2002, a road map to join the EU was agreed; the country joined NATO two years later; and 2007 was fixed as the year of miraculous salvation when Bulgaria would become a full member of the EU. Watch this space.

⬤ *Detail from the façade of the National Theatre*

Lifestyle

The lifestyle encountered in the city centre is recognisably that of continental Europe, characterised by a predominantly young population, with familiar brand names in the shop windows and advertisements for mobile phones. The pace of life may be slower than what you are used to, and there is a pleasantly relaxed start to working days; weekends, by comparison, seem comatose. Young people learn English as their second language (their parents learned Russian), and their general level of education is high. While you cannot assume that English is generally understood, young people working in hotels and restaurants understand your needs and are usually more than willing to help.

While the lifestyle is Western European – and with a hedonistic vengeance when it comes to pavement cafés and bars – one aspect of Sofia that is decidedly Eastern is the alphabet. Sofia uses the Cyrillic alphabet, as used in Russia, the Ukraine and Serbia. What will confuse you is that although some of the 30 letters look the same as Latin ones, they are pronounced very differently. A typical example is the word ресторант – which you will be tempted to read as 'pectopaht' – which means 'restaurant'. The briefest look at the Cyrillic alphabet (see page 52) will pay dividends when it comes to deciphering street and place names.

There is another lifestyle in Sofia, the one lived by an older generation that has had to cope with the momentous changes associated with the transition from a state-governed economy to a capitalist one, and the shift from a Balkan to a more Western European culture. It can be observed and appreciated in the Women's Market in the centre of the city – this is where ordinary people come to buy their clothes, food and other provisions – and here you will see the older lifestyle still ticking away. Shoppers in the market know how to judge the freshness of the fruits and vegetables on the stalls and they know the value of every stotinki (a hundred of which make up one lev, the unit of the currency). To enjoy and understand Sofia means acknowledging both these lifestyles.

🔺 *Graffiti comes in Cyrillic, too*

Culture

The decades of subjugation under authoritarian, pro-Soviet governments fostered aspects of cultural development that were seen as intrinsically worthwhile but not threatening to the status quo. The legacy of this is that Sofia is home to a wealth of musical and theatrical establishments and, although the visitor that doesn't understand Bulgarian is handicapped when it comes to drama, there are wonderful opportunities to enjoy opera, ballet and classical music. Spring, when musical festivities get underway, is the best time to enjoy these art forms although whatever the time of year, ticket prices are always wonderfully affordable. The Sofia Philharmonic Orchestra performs regularly, and the National Opera has seating for 1,200 and a repertoire of internationally recognised operas and ballets. Musicals and operettas from around the world are performed, from *Die Fledermaus* to *Evita*, and although performances are in Bulgarian they can still be hugely enjoyable if you are familiar with the piece.

Bulgaria's traditional culture is well represented at the National Ethnographical Museum, housed in the former Royal Palace, which also plays host to international exhibitions. The most important collections, principally Thracian gold and silver treasures, have their home at the National History Museum, situated at Boyana, to the south of the city, although the Thracian collection is often out of the country. In the same neighbourhood stands Boyana Church, famous for its fragile frescoes from the medieval age. Back in the city centre, the National Archaeological Museum has a number of interesting finds that date back to the time of ancient Greece and Rome.

● *Check out the sculptures at the Puta Gallery*

The architecture in Sofia is one of the delights freely available to the stroller, and there is an unusual mix that takes in Byzantine-inspired churches and Soviet-influenced socialist art. The former headquarters of the Central Committee of the Communist Party still asserts itself, architecturally anyway, and only a short walk away stands the grand Alexander Nevsky Memorial Church, designed by a Russian architect in a neo-Byzantine style, and home to a superb collection of icons from around the country. Equally impressive is the art nouveau interior of the city's synagogue, eloquent testimony to Bulgaria's tremendous act of saving its Jews in World War II, and the aesthetically effective Soviet Army Monument. The icing on the architectural cake takes high-spirited form in the neo-wacky Russian Church, built in 1913 for an ultra devout diplomat from the soon-to-be-toppled Tsarist empire.

The National Art Gallery is in Sofia, but many visitors find more engaging art work in the National Gallery of Foreign Art and in smaller establishments like the City Art Gallery where changing exhibitions are likely to offer something interesting. New artistic endeavours, especially in painting and sculpture, are also to be found in a number of small, private galleries dotted around the city. In these galleries, original art work is for sale and often at very agreeable prices. This art scene is a shifting and ongoing one, but the relevant sections of the free city guides will highlight new galleries that have opened up and attracted attention.

Clashing architectural styles in Nezavisimost Square

Shopping

Shopping is an art form of its own in Sofia, and to find something interesting you often need to hunt down individual shops and stores. Fashionable Vitosha Boulevard, in the heart of the city, is a concentrated shopping area, particularly for clothing. It is pedestrianised, and so ideal for window shopping; a drawback for some, however, is that the outlets tend to focus on familiar Western brands. The same is true of Tzum, now a modern shopping mall, but once the state-owned department store justified its name 'central

USEFUL SHOPPING PHRASES

What time do the shops open/close?
В колко часа отварят/затварят магазините?
V kolko chasa otvaryat/zatvaryat magazinite?

How much is this?
Колко струва това?
Kolko struva tova?

Can I try this on?
Може ли да го пробвам?
Mozhe li da go probvam?

My size is ...
Моят размер е ...
Moyat razmer eh ...

I'll take this one, thank you.
Ще взема този, благодаря.
Shte vzema tozi, blagodarya.

This is too large/too small/too expensive.
Do you have any others?
Това е много голямо/малко/скъпо. Имате ли други?
Tova eh mnogo golyamo/malko/skapo. Imateh li drugi?

universal shop' (the Bulgarian for which renders the abbreviated form 'Tzum').

More rewarding in many ways is the narrow Shishman Street, easy to find because it starts next to the Radisson hotel, and home to a number of small, proprietor-run shops. As with Vitosha Boulevard, the emphasis is on clothing but the boutiques are more individual and each place has its own tiny but unique collection. Across Sofia as a whole, boutiques for women easily outnumber their counterparts for men.

Pedestrianised Pirotska Street, where there are more boutiques, leads to the southern end of Zhenski Pazar, the Women's Market. Crammed with stalls and shoppers, this is the place to buy a jar of fresh honey or stock up on your supply of vegetable seeds. The best market of all, in terms of finding something to bring home, is in front of the Alexander Nevsky Memorial Church.

For original Bulgarian art, the area worth exploring is around Parizh Street, close to the Alexander Nevsky Memorial Church and the National Opera. Here you will find a number of small galleries promoting the work of a new generation of young artists who work in a variety of styles from the expressive to the pictorial. An export licence may be required for some purchases, but the shops can arrange this.

An increasing number of shops will accept credit cards, and the relevant logos will be visible by the entrance or the till, but you may come across places that do not and the only option is to pay by cash.

⬤ Matryoshka *dolls for sale at the Alexander Nevsky Square market*

Eating & drinking

It is never a problem finding somewhere to eat and drink in Sofia. Prices are remarkably low, and often the more traditional Bulgarian dishes are preferable to Western European favourites. Standards of service vary, and you can be very pleased one day only to return another time and experience poor service, delays and confusion; this is all part of the city's learning curve rather than culpable lapses in standards. As a general rule, be as explicit as possible and try to check that your order has been understood.

Just about every menu begins with a list of various salads and among these there is nearly always a *shopska*. Almost a national dish, a *shopska* is made with chopped tomatoes, cucumber, peppers and onion, topped with white cheese. The *ovcharska* salad is similar but comes with grated egg and mushrooms. Equally popular is *snezhanka*, chopped cucumber with garlic mixed together in yogurt. For vegetarians, one of the salads followed by a hot starter makes a suitable meal at lunchtime. Hot starters feature stuffed or roasted peppers and tend to avoid meat.

Soups feature on most menus and the ones most likely to appear include *bob chorba* (bean soup) and *shkembe chorba* (tripe soup). Vegetarians should look for *tarator* in the warm months – a refreshing, cold soup composed of yogurt and cucumber.

Main courses are usually based around meat, with chicken, pork and veal being the firm favourites, and grilled meats are very common. Expect to find *kyufteta* (meat balls), *parzhola* (chops) and *kebapcheta* (elongated meat balls). The choice of fish can be

● *Vitosha Boulevard from the Upstairs bar*

disappointing and usually comes down to *pasturva* (trout) and the seasonal offering from the Black Sea. Desserts are a real let-down, and finding yourself tempted by wicked chocolate concoctions is, sadly, all too rare an experience. However, ice cream is popular and of good quality.

Sofia has no shortage of places to drink, and even the humblest café or kiosk tends to stock a range of soft drinks, beers and spirits. Cappuccinos feature on many menus, but prepare to be disappointed when a powdery substance stirred limply into life with a modicum of froth arrives on your table. Regular coffee, often just called American, may be too strong or just plain dire. Tea is widely available but unless you specifically ask for black tea (*cheren chayi*), you will receive a herbal teabag without milk.

The most popular spirit is *rakiya*, a brandy made from plums, grapes or apricots. It is traditionally drunk with a salad as an aperitif and, with 40 per cent alcohol, packs a punch. *Rakiya* and other spirits are listed in menus as 'small' (50 g/1³/₄ oz and roughly equivalent to a British double) or 'large' (100 g/3¹/₂ oz), and there is often a variety of brands and prices to choose from. Burgas 63 is a good brand of *rakiya* for both plum and grape varieties; *Troyanska*

> ### RESTAURANT PRICE RATING
> The following approximate price bands are based on the average cost of a three-course meal for one person, excluding drinks, and are indicated by these symbols:
> **£** under 15lv; **££** above 15lv and less than 30lv; **£££** more than 30lv
> In even the most expensive restaurants, you would seriously need to push the boat out in order to pay more than 50lv for a three-course meal.

one of the better plum brandies; and *Peshterska muskatova* is a good grape equivalent.

Bulgarian wines are not as bad as you might suspect, and familiar grapes like Merlot and Cabernet Sauvignon have been grown with notable success. Mavrud is a Bulgarian grape variety, and the wine is worth tasting if you like a beefsteak quality to your wine. Bulgarian beers are palatable but not habit-forming, and imported Danish, German and Czech beers are commonly available.

🔺 *A traditional* shopska *salad, smothered in cheese*

USEFUL DINING PHRASES

I would like a table for ... people.
Бих искал маса за ... души.
Bih iskal masa za ... dushi.

May I have the bill, please?
Сметката, моля?
Smetkata, molya?

Waiter/waitress!
Келнер!
Kelner!

Could I have it well-cooked/medium/rare please?
Може ли да го приготвите добре опечено/средно опечено, моля?
Mozhe li da go prigotvite dobre opecheno/sredno opecheno, molya?

I am a vegetarian. Does this contain meat?
Аз съм вегетарианец. Има ли месо тук?
Az sm vegetarianets. Ima li mesoh tuk?

Where is the toilet (restroom) please?
Къде е тоалетната, моля?
Kadeh eh toaletnata, molya?

I would like a cup of/two cups of/another coffee/tea.
Искам чаша/две чаши/още една чаша кафе/чай.
Iskam chasha/dve chashi/oshteh edna chasha kafeh/chai.

PRACTICALITIES

Most restaurants are open seven days a week from between 10.00 and 11.00 onwards, closing around 23.00 or later. A service charge is not usually added to the bill and a tip of 10 per cent is normally expected. By law, all restaurants should have a designated non-smoking area, but this is invariably a nominal affair. Wine lists in restaurants tend to be based around Bulgarian wines, and only the more expensive places will feature international selections. Half bottles are rarely listed on menus, but most places have no problem serving their wines by the glass. Meal prices are remarkably low by Western European standards and this goes some way in compensating for inconsistencies in standards and service.

⬤ *A typical street café*

Entertainment & nightlife

Sofia's entertainment scene is broadly night-based and you will be surprised at the sheer number of bars, nightclubs and pubs that light up after dark and remain busy until the early hours of the morning. There is the usual gamut of so-called Irish pubs and Buddha bars, but it is more interesting to seek out some of the small bars and clubs, like O! Shipka, where young Bulgarians party away the night, and up-and-coming musicians try to make a breakthrough. Piano bars are popular in a low-key kind of way, and provide a musical alternative to loud doses of pop rock. There are no cover charges in the clubs, and there is usually a drinks list in English. The Bulgarian for 'cheers' is *nazdrave*, meaning 'good health' and, if you find yourself in a group toasting, etiquette demands that you clink your glass with each and every person in the group.

Bulgarian folk music usually takes the form of *chalga* – shaking up the body and waggling limbs to a hybrid ethno-pop sound. In visitor-oriented restaurants, like Sheherezada, staff are decked out in *Arabian Nights* costumes, but the shows are not as tacky as you might fear. Where some caution should be exercised is with the more lurid-looking nightclubs that obviously aim to draw in an adult male audience; it is not unknown for a hapless punter to be landed with a heavy bill and given no option but to pay up. The casinos that announce their presence in neon are best only patronised by the experienced.

Check out ⓦ www.programata.bg for current listings of entertainment, nightlife and cultural events.

There are wonderful opportunities to enjoy Sofia's interest in ballet and classical music – one of the legacies of the Soviet era – and the free listings magazines carry details of current shows and performances. The main venue is the National Palace of Culture (often referred to as the NDK from its name in Bulgarian – Natsionalen Dvorets na Kulturata) with its 3,800-seat main hall and many smaller concert spaces. Throughout the year, it hosts a variety of cultural events (see pages 10–11). Bulgaria Hall in Aksakov Street (see page 75) is home to the Bulgarian Philharmonic. The National

▲ *Sofia Garden, home to the National Theatre and Bulgaria Hall*

Opera and Ballet performs in Vrabcha Street (see page 88), and musicals and operettas also take place in the National Musical Theatre in Vassil Levski Boulevard. Tickets for ballet and music, which are amazingly affordable compared to Western Europe, can be booked in advance at the box offices of the various theatres. Usual opening hours are 10.00–18.30 (sometimes closed between 13.30 and 15.30).

CINEMA

Hollywood films, with subtitles in Bulgarian, are shown regularly in cinemas, and ticket prices average about 7lv. Seats can be booked in advance, and should be at weekends. The main cinema complex, with eight screens, is underneath the NDK (☎ (02) 951 5101). A new cineplex is about to open at the City Centre Sofia shopping mall just beyond the NDK centre (⌖ Cherni Vrah Boulevard Ⓝ Tram: No 9).

LISTINGS

The Insider's Guide is a free listings magazine that appears every three months, and copies should be available in your hotel. There is also a free monthly *City Info Guide* that covers the same ground. Both these guides carry their own useful maps of the city area. Every Friday, the English-language *Sofia Echo* appears and carries current listings of what's on at the cinemas and details of theatrical and musical events.

See Ⓦ www.programata.bg for current information on Sofia's cultural, entertainment and nightlife scene.

⊙ *Statue of Alexander Stamboliyski, 1920s prime minister, outside the National Opera House*

Sport & relaxation

With an altitude of 1,800 m (5,906 ft), Bulgaria's highest mountain resort is Mount Vitosha, only 22 km (13½ miles) away from the city centre and reachable by a bus ride. Between December and April, thick snow cover provides good ski runs – with a total length of 29 km (18 miles) – that serve both beginners and the experienced. There is a ski school at Aleko, situated just above the tree line, that teaches absolute beginners from the age of six upwards, and all the gear can be hired by the day. Outside of winter, the area is popular with hikers, and trails criss-cross the mountain. There is a chair-lift from the village suburb of Dragalevtsi as well as Simeonovo. On the more wooded western side of the mountain, Zlatni mostove is an outdoor area that is a good picnic spot in the summer. If you go there on a weekday, you will have plenty of space to yourself and you can explore the huge boulders that line the course of the river.

Sofia has a number of parks, but the one that offers the most in the way of relaxation is Borisova Gradina. This is the largest park in the city, and an hour or more could easily be spent wandering its paths; it is also suitable for jogging. The stadium in the park belongs to the Bulgarian Army club team, CKSA (❶ (02) 963 3477), one of the city's two most important soccer teams. The other team, Levski, plays at the Stadion Georgi Asparuhov in the northeast of the city (❶ (02) 989 2156). Tickets do not need to be bought in advance and are available at the grounds on the day of a match. Important and international matches are played at the Vasil Levski Stadium in Borisova Gradina (❶ (02) 988 5030).

There is a bowling alley in town at Galaxy Bowling (❸ Bulgaria Boulevard 1 ❶ (02) 916 6590 ❹ 11.00–24.00), and out of town at the 18-alley Mexa Xtreme Bowling Centre (❸ Akadermik Boris Stefanov

12 in Studentski Grad ☎ (02) 969 2600 ⏰ 12.00–04.00). Nearby, in Prof Atanas Ishirkov, the ice rink at the Winter Sport Palace is open until mid-April and skates can be rented.

● *Snowboarders waiting for the bus to Mount Vitosha*

Accommodation

There is a good range of accommodation in Sofia, from hostels to 5-star opulence, and you should be able to stay close to the city centre. Some good, mid-range hotels, like the Lozenetz, are just a little outside the city centre but still within walking distance – a tram ride or an inexpensive taxi-ride away. Expect some quirks as even the best hotels can fail when it comes to brown bread for breakfast, and a toaster may be missing from an otherwise good 3-star place. This sounds like carping, but prices are comparable to Western European ones where standards are higher.

It is best to make internet bookings in advance, either directly with the hotel or through an accommodation website like Ⓦ www.sofiahotels.net or Ⓦ www.hotelsinsofia.com. A buffet breakfast is included in the room rates. Tea- and coffee-making facilities are not usually available in hotel rooms, but mini-bars are in many mid-range hotels, and a safety deposit box is either in the room or available at reception. English-speaking staff in all the hotels listed here are usually very helpful when it comes to calling a taxi for you or dealing with day-to-day enquiries.

ACCOMMODATION PRICE RATINGS

The following price guides indicate the approximate cost of a room for two people for one night, including tax and breakfast unless otherwise stated.

£ under 150lv/€75; ££ Above 150lv/€75 and under 300lv/€150; £££ Above 300lv/€150

Baldjieva £ Centrally located off Vitosha Boulevard, this hotel has eight rather plain rooms, but offers affordable rates and a comfortable night's sleep. ⓐ Tsar Assen Street 23 ⓣ (02) 981 1257 ⓦ www.baldjievahotel.net

Be My Guest £ Dorms and double rooms spread about a funkily decorated hostel; good central location. ⓐ Ivan Vazov Street 13 ⓣ (02) 989 5092 ⓦ www.bemyguest-hostel.com

California £ Such a lovely place, though a little outside the centre in Lozenets. A variety of rooms plus sauna, room service, internet access and a restaurant in traditional Bulgarian style. ⓐ Bigla Street 30 ⓣ (02) 962 9300 ⓕ (02) 962 5542 ⓦ www.hotelcaliforniasofia.com

HostelMostel £ Bunk-bed accommodation in dorms in a hostel with more living space than Be My Guest (see above). Popular hostel where floor space is also available if you have your own sleeping bag. ⓐ Denkoglu 2 ⓣ 0889 223296 ⓦ www.hostelmostel.com

Internet Hostel £ In the heart of the city; nicely decorated, private rooms, decent kitchen, internet access. ⓐ Alabin Street 50 ⓣ 0888 384828 ⓔ interhostel@yahoo.co.uk

Kervan Hostel £ Comfortable and cosy hostel to the north of Alexander Nevsky Memorial Church and close to the Opera House. ⓐ Rositsa Street 3 ⓣ (02) 983 9428 ⓦ www.kervanhostel.com

Pop Bogomil £ Situated in an area of cobbled streets and close to the city centre. Rooms are smallish and decorated a little kookily, but are basically comfortable. Breakfast costs only a little extra and rooms with a bath need requesting in advance. ⓐ Pop Bogomil 5 ① (02) 983 1165 ① (02) 983 7065 ② hotelpopbogomil@dir.bg

Red Bed and Breakfast £ Part of the building that houses the Red House cultural centre, this is a good B&B where breakfast is brought to your room and where a pleasant terrace on the top floor offers space for relaxing on warm summer evenings. ⓐ Lyuben Karavelov 15 ① (02) 988 8188 ⓦ www.redbandb.com

Sveta Sofia £ Attractive and central location. ⓐ Pirotska Street 18 ① (02) 917 9090 ① (02) 983 1723 ⓦ www.svetasofia-alexanders.com

Tzar Asen £ Seven rooms in a quiet suburban setting. ⓐ Tsar Assen Street 68 ① (02) 954 7801 ⓦ www.hotel-tzar-asen.hit.bg

Niky £–££ Quiet location off Vitosha Boulevard, with good-value singles and doubles plus 17 suites with kitchenettes. Well run, helpful staff, free internet and pleasant restaurant (see page 97). ⓐ Neofit Rilski Street 16 ① (02) 851 1915 ① (02) 951 6091 ⓦ www.hotel-niky.com

Rodina £–££ A huge hotel, some 330 rooms and plenty of singles, as well as four restaurants and three bars. ⓐ Totleben Boulevard 8 ① (02) 917 9999 ① (02) 951 5840 ⓦ www.rodina.bg

Art 'Otel ££ One block away from Vitosha Boulevard, this hotel has over 20 rooms, some of which offer cityscape views. ⓐ Gladston Street 44 ① (02) 980 6000 ① (02) 981 1909 ⓦ www.artotel.biz

Central ££ On the west side of the city with 25 rooms that have wireless internet access. Bar, restaurant, sauna and laundry service. **ⓐ** Hristo Botev Boulevard 52 **ⓣ** (02) 981 2364 **ⓕ** (02) 986 4561 **ⓦ** www.central-hotel.com

Central Forum ££ Rooms are adequate but only the more expensive ones have baths as well as showers; some have electric kettles as well. Good central location. **ⓐ** Tsar Boris III 43 **ⓣ** (02) 954 4444 **ⓕ** (02) 954 3333 **ⓦ** www.central-hotel.com

△ *The wide open space of Vitosha Boulevard*

Diter ££ A smart hotel in a quiet location with excellent facilities, including safe and mini-bar. Well managed; restaurant downstairs. ⓐ Han Asparuh 65 ⓣ (02) 989 8998 ⓦ www.diterhotel.com

Light ££ Located in a quiet, cobbled street but central; a touch of class in the contemporary décor but most rooms have only a shower. ⓐ Veslets Street 37 ⓣ (02) 917 9090 ⓕ (02) 917 9010 ⓦ www.hotellight.com

Lozenetz ££ Just south of the city centre, this is a modern and classy hotel with a good restaurant, friendly staff and wireless connections. ⓐ Sv Naum Street 23 ⓣ (02) 965 4444 ⓕ (02) 965 4445 ⓦ www.lozenetzhotel.com

Serdika ££ A 3-star hotel in the Communist era and now coming in at a similar pitch with reasonable single and double rooms. ⓐ Yanko Sakuzov Boulevard ⓣ (02) 919 3636 ⓕ (02) 944 3619 ⓦ www.serdikahotel.com

Crystal Palace £££ One of the best hotels in the city, in a quiet location but close to the centre. It has a health and fitness club with sauna, internet connections in the rooms, and an above-average restaurant (see page 87). ⓐ Shipska Street 14 ⓣ (02) 948 9488 ⓦ www.crystalpalace-sofia.com

Hilton Hotel £££ Reliably first class, with free use of pool and gym, and a good restaurant; situated behind the NDK. ⓐ Bulgaria Boulevard 1 ⓣ (02) 933 5000 ⓕ (02) 933 5111 ⓦ www.sofia.hilton.com

Radisson SAS £££ A great location opposite Alexander Nevsky Memorial Church, and one of the best places to stay. Wireless connections everywhere in the hotel; comfortable and stylish rooms.
ⓐ Narodno Sabranie 4 ⓣ (02) 933 4334 ⓕ (02) 933 4335
ⓦ www.sofia.radissonsas.com

Sheraton Sofia Hotel Balkan £££ A landmark hotel when it opened in the mid-1950s to serve dignitaries and politicos; now a classic with its high ceilings, marble columns and stately staircases.
ⓐ Sveta Nedelya Square ⓣ (02) 981 6541 ⓕ (02) 980 6464
ⓦ www.luxurycollection.com

🔺 *The elegant Sheraton Sofia*

THE BEST OF SOFIA

TOP 10 ATTRACTIONS

- **Alexander Nevsky Memorial Church** Neo-Byzantine extravaganza and, outside, a great street market (see pages 76–7).

- **Borisova Gradina** Sofia's largest park with ponds and paths and non-urban vibes (see pages 104–5).

- **Sushi and a boogie at the Bibliotekata** Underneath the National Library, a sushi bar and live music (see page 86).

- **Frescoes in Boyana Church** Unique frescoes from the 13th century, comparable to the achievements of the early Italian Renaissance (see pages 106–7).

- **Rila Monastery** Bulgaria's best monastery – a day trip from Sofia (see page 120).

- **Sofia's pub-restaurants** A plethora of alfresco bars serving food through a long summer's night.

- **The Women's Market** Balkan flavours in Sofia's most traditional market (see pages 65–6).

- **Skiing and/or hiking around Mount Vitosha** The snow-capped mountain seen from the city centre (see page 119).

- **O! Shipka** Garden restaurant and, below stairs, indie music from a new generation (see page 111).

- **Sofia Synagogue** Spanish-Moorish style and, wait for it, the biggest chandelier in the Balkans (see page 66).

◗ *Bulgarians and Russians meeting in victory, 1945*

What do you do with a limited amount of time?

HALF-DAY: SOFIA IN A HURRY

There is enough time to walk the city centre and see the main sights. Start outside the Radisson SAS hotel and cross the cobbled square, past the white parliament building, to the Alexander Nevsky Memorial Church and its golden domes. The crypt houses a priceless collection of icons, while out in the public square vendors retail World War II memorabilia and assorted artefacts. A short walk westwards, along Tsar Osvoboditel Boulevard, passes the stunning little Russian church and its five golden onion domes, then the National Art Gallery and the Ethnographic Museum. A little further on is Alexander Batenberg Square, where troops once goose-stepped and tanks rolled by in convoys during the Stalinist era. Appropriately enough, you soon find yourself gazing up at the colonnaded Party House, former headquarters of the Communist Party. You are now on the west side of the city and close to Halite, with a choice of places to eat (see page 72).

ONE DAY: TIME TO SEE A LITTLE MORE

The half-day itinerary above could be followed, after leaving Halite, by a visit to the city's attractive synagogue and then a stroll down the pedestrianised Pirotska Street, which leads to the Women's Market. You may purchase very little, but the authentic flavour of the Balkans is gradually disappearing in the capital and it can still be experienced for real here. There is also time for a quick walk past the church of Sveta Nedelya and a look at the shops in Vitosha Boulevard. You could end the day in style by enjoying a Bulgarian-style meal at the elegant Crystal Palace hotel and taking a short stroll down the street to the bar and nightclub at O! Shipka.

2–3 DAYS: SHORT CITY-BREAK

The first day, or day and a half, could be occupied with the suggestions opposite, while the extra time would allow for a day trip out of the city centre to the National History Museum or Boyana Church. It takes only an hour to reach Mount Vitosha, and you would also have time for a day's skiing or a hike on the mountain. The nights give you time to drop in on some more of the city's bars and restaurants.

LONGER: ENJOYING SOFIA TO THE FULL

You can do all of the above and still have time to experience the full Top 10 Attractions (see pages 42–3). Spend a day exploring bucolic Koprivshtitsa and the town's traditional Bulgarian architecture and/or, in a more hedonistic spirit, take an excursion to the bars of Blagoevgrad. A trip to fortress-like Rila Monastery could also be on your itinerary.

⬣ Party House, former HQ of the Communist Party

Something for nothing

Sofia's great churches are free to enter and so you can explore
Alexander Nevsky Memorial Church (though there is a small charge
to view the crypt), the **Church of St George** behind the Sheraton
hotel, **Sveta Nedelya Church** and **St Nicholas Russian Church** at your
leisure. The **National Gallery for Foreign Art** is free on Mondays. The
city's parks are free, and **Borisova Gradina** always makes a relaxing
destination on a fine day. **Yuzhen Park** is not a very green space, and
Sofia City Garden is a more peaceful place to take a rest; if you fancy
your chess skills, feel free to challenge one of the players who
regularly uses part of the park.

Sofia has a compact city centre and the following walk costs
nothing but takes in many sights. Start outside Sveta Nedelya
Church and walk north up Maria Luiza Boulevard to Pirotska Street.
Walk down pedestrianised Pirotska Street and at the end turn to the
right to enter the **Women's Market**. After exploring the market,
retrace your steps to Maria Luisa Boulevard and cross to the other
side, and head back the way you came. After passing the giant Tzum
shopping mall, turn left into Nezavisimost Square, and you
immediately see the magisterial **Party House** looming ahead. Cross
to the other side so that you keep Party House on your left as you
walk into Alexander Batenberg Square and the City Garden on your
right. There is a large open-air café-bar that opens in the summer
opposite the National Theatre in the park. After a rest in the park,
walk back to Alexander Batenberg Square and, facing the park, the
former royal palace that now houses an art gallery and museum.
A short walk eastwards along Tsar Osvoboditel Boulevard brings you
to the delightful St Nicholas Russian Church. Continue along the
boulevard until you come to the Radisson SAS hotel and Narodino

Sabranie Square. From here you can see the Alexander Nevsky Memorial Church on your left. After leaving the church continue eastwards along Tsar Osvoboditel Boulevard and cross to the other side to enter Borisova Gradina. Head for the **Monument to the Soviet Army** to admire the best piece of public art in Sofia.

⏺ *Frieze around the base of the Monument to the Soviet Army*

When it rains

All the churches and museums can be visited on a wet day and, as many of them are close to one another, you need only an umbrella to keep safely dry. From the **Alexander Nevsky Memorial Church** it takes less than five minutes to reach the **Russian Church** and, almost next door, the **National Art Gallery** and the **Ethnographic Museum** are conveniently together in a former royal palace. Opposite the Russian Church there is a comfortable café to enjoy a break, and from the café it is a five-minute walk to the **Archaeological Museum**. The **Sofia Synagogue**, the **Banya Bashi Mosque** and the church of **Sveta Nedelya** are also near one another, and time inside these buildings could be combined with some window shopping in the Tzum shopping mall and, across the street, Halite, where food and drink is also available.

A wet day provides an opportunity to visit some of the smaller museums and galleries dotted around the city. The **Ivan Vazov Museum** is in the house where the author lived and is a period piece in its own right; there are also bars and restaurants very close by. The foyer of the **Russian cultural centre** on Shipka Street is home to a virtually life-size model of the Vostok-3 capsule that sent Yuri Gagarin into space

By way of entertainment, a visit to the **cinema** will escape the rain and, if you head for the one in the NDK underpass in Yuzhen Park, you will also find a café-bar in the foyer. The other main cinema complex, in the City Centre Sofia shopping mall, is a short walk from behind the Hilton hotel.

A trip to the **National History Museum** would take up at least half of one wet day although, to avoid the rain, a taxi ride there and back would be best. Whatever the weather, Sofia's countless bars are always open, and if you stayed in the vicinity of **Tsar Ivan Shishman Street**, it would be easy to pop from one to another without getting too wet.

🔺 *Dodge the rain showers at the Banya Bashi Mosque*

On arrival

TIME DIFFERENCES

Sofia is two hours ahead of Greenwich Mean Time (GMT) and seven hours ahead of Eastern Standard Time (EST). When it is 12.00 in Sofia, it is 10.00 in London, 05.00 in New York, 02.00 in Los Angeles and 20.00 in Sydney. During Bulgarian summer time, clocks are put forward one hour between the beginning of April and the end of October.

ARRIVING

Arriving by air

Sofia International Airport, 10 km (7 miles) east of the city centre, is small for a European capital but the basic facilities are provided: ATM, exchange bureau, car hire, café and a desk for booking a taxi with OK Supertrans (in front of you to the right as you enter the arrivals hall). Ignore the taxi touts and, after using the ATM machine, book a taxi for the short journey into town. The fare will be between 7lv and 10lv. Between 05.00 and 23.00, bus No 84 runs to Orlov Most, east of the city centre, from a bus stop outside the airport, 100 m (110 yds) to the right; you need to purchase a ticket (0.50lv) from the kiosk near the bus stop before boarding the bus (see page 56).

Arriving by train

Sofia's Central Station (☎ (02) 931 1111 ⊛ www.bdz.bg
🕒 05.00–24.00) is an ugly concrete shelter north of the city centre on Mariya Luiza Boulevard. It is 20 minutes away on foot or by tram Nos 1 or 7 to/from Sveta Nedelya Square (purchase ticket for 0.50lv from the kiosk before boarding). ATMs and left-luggage facilities are

available at the station. Beware of meter scams from taxi drivers hanging around the station; it may be worth walking the short distance to the bus station and catching one there.

Arriving by bus
The **Central Bus Station** (Ⓦ www.geology.bas.bg/sofia.html), 200 m (219 yds) east of the railway station on Mariya Luiza Boulevard, is a well-organised place with good facilities, including ATMs, left-luggage facility, food court, information desk and a taxi-booking kiosk. For public transport into town, walk to the train station for tram Nos 1 or 7.

IF YOU GET LOST, TRY ...

Excuse me, do you speak English?
Извинете, говорите ли английски?
Izvinete, govorite li angleeski?

Excuse me, is this the right way to ... the cathedral/the tourist office/the castle/the old town?
Извинете, това ли е пътят за ... катедралата/туристическото бюро/замъка/стария град?
Izvinete, tova li eh puhtyat za ... katedralata/turisticheskoto byuro/zamuhka/stariya grad?

Can you point to it on my map?
Може ли да ми покажете на моята карта?
Mozhe li da mi pokazhete na moyata karta?

THE CYRILLIC ALPHABET

А а	a as in cat	П п	p as in pot
Б б	b as in bus	Р р	r as in rasp
В в	v as in very	С с	s as in see
Г г	g as in go	Т т	t as in tip
Д д	d as in door	У у	u as in rule
Е е	e as in bet	Ф ф	f as in fruit
Ж ж	zh like the s in leisure	Х х	ch as in loch
З з	z as in zoo	Ц ц	ts as in shut
И и	i as in bit	Ч ч	ch as in chip
Й й	y as in yes	Ш ш	sh as in ship
К к	k as in kit	Щ щ	sht like the last
Л л	l as in like		syllable joshed
М м	m as in met	Ъ ъ	u as in but
Н н	n as in net	Ю ю	yu as in you
О о	o as in got	Я я	ya as in yarn

FINDING YOUR FEET

Sofia is a safe city to travel around and the pace of life is not frantic. The difficulty is grappling with the Cyrillic alphabet. Finding a menu in English is not difficult, but a sign or street name is more elusive, and it is good to have at least a nodding acquaintance with the alphabet.

ORIENTATION

The use of the Cyrillic alphabet for street names makes orientation a little more difficult than it would otherwise be, and it pays to study a map before setting out for any destination. If you get confused about which street you are on, ask someone for directions – a young person is more likely to speak English – or enquire in a shop. The main tram routes, marked on the map, are often helpful in orientating yourself, and major landmarks include the National

⬤ РЕСТОРАНТ ГРОЗД = *RESTAURANT GROZD*

Trams stops are sometimes in the middle of the road and passengers wait on the pavement until the tram approaches.

Getting around by taxi

Registered taxis, painted bright yellow, are easy to find and use digital meters. There are disreputable taxi companies that will overcharge, but as long as you use the companies listed here there should be no problem. The driver's ID card, car number and table of fares should be clearly displayed – currently around 0.50lv per

⬧ Many different vehicles have to share the road

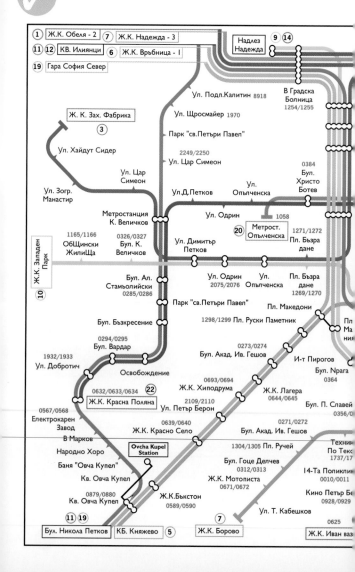

① Ж.К. Обеля - 2 ⑦ Ж.К. Надежда - 3 ⑨ ⑭ Надлез Надежда

⑪ ⑫ КВ. Илиянци ⑥ Ж.К. Връбница - I

⑲ Гара София Север

Ул. Подп.Калитин 8918

В Градска Болница 1254/1255

Ул. Щросмайер 1970

Ж. К. Зах. Фабрика
③

Парк "св.Петъри Павел"

Ул. Хайдут Сидер

2249/2250
Ул. Цар Симеон

Ул. Зогр. Манастир

Ул. Цар Симеон

Ул. Д.Петков

Ул. Опълченска

0384
Бул. Христо Ботев

Метростанция К. Величков

Ул. Одрин 1058

⑳ Метрост. Опълченска

1271/1272
Пл. Бъзра дане

1165/1166
ОбЩински ЖилиЩа

0326/0327
Бул. К. Величков

Ул. Димитър Петков

⑩ Ж.К. Западен Парк

Бул. Ал. Стамболийски
0285/0286

Ул. Одрин
2075/2076

Ул. Опълченска

Пл. Бъзра дане
1269/1270

Парк "св.Петъри Павел"

Бул. Бъзкресение

1298/1299 Пл. Руски Паметник

Пл Ма ния

0294/0295
Бул. Вардар

Бул. Акад. Ив. Гешов

1932/1933
Ул. Добротич

0273/0274

И-т Пирогов

Бул. Npaгa
0364

Освобождение

0693/0694
Ж.К. Хиподрума

Ж.К. Лагера
0644/0645

Бул. П. Славей
0356/0

0632/0633/0634 ㉒
Ж.К. Красна Поляна

2109/2110
Ул. Петър Берон

0639/0640
Ж.К. Красно Село

Бул. Акад. Ив. Гешов
0271/0272

0567/0568
Електрокарен Завод

В Марков

1304/1305 Пл. Ручей

Техничи По Текс
1737/17

Народно Хоро

Бул. Гоце Делчев
0312/0313

14-Та Поликлин
0010/0011

Баня "Овча Купел"

Ovcha Kupel Station

Ж.К. Мотолиста
0671/0672

Кино Петър Бе
0928/0929

Кв. Овча Купел

0879/0880
Кв. Овча Купел

Ж.К.Бъкстон
0589/0590

Ул. Т. Кабешков

0625

⑪ ⑲ Бул. Никола Петков КБ. Княжево ⑤ Ж.К. Борово Ж.К. Иван ваз

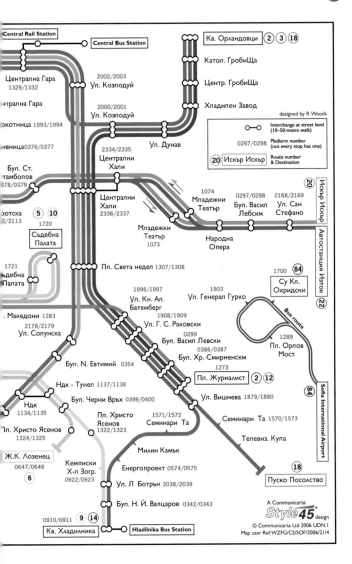

Central Rail Station
Central Bus Station

Централна Гара
1329/1332

...нтральна Гара

...окотница 1993/1994

...ивница 0376/0377

Бул. Ст.
...тамболов
...378/0379

...оотска ⑤ ⑩
.../2113

Съдебна
Палата

1721
...ьдебна
Палата

. Македони 1283

2178/2179
Ул. Солунска

Ндк

Ндк - Тунел 1137/1138

Бул. N. Евтимий 0354

Бул. Черни Връх 0399/0400

1134/1135

Пл. Христо Ясенов
1324/1325

Ж.К. Лозенец
0647/0648
⑥

2002/2003
Ул. Козлодуй

2000/2001
Ул. Козлодуй

Централни
Хали
2334/2335

Централни
Хали
2336/2337

Пл. Света недел 1307/1308

1996/1997
Ул. Кн. Ал.
Батемберг

1908/1909
Ул. Г. С. Раковски

0299
Бул. Васил Левски

0386/0387
Бул. Хр. Смирненскм

Пл. Христо
Ясенов
1322/1323

1571/1572
Семинари Та

Милин Камък

Кемписки
Х-л Зогр.
0922/0923

Энергопроект 0574/0575

Ул. Л Ботрън 2038/2039

Бул. Н. Й. Вапцаров 0342/0343

0910/0911 ⑨ ⑭
Кв. Хладилника
Hladilnika Bus Station

Кв. Орландовци ②③⑱

Катол. ГробиЩа

Центр. ГробиЩа

Хладилен Завод

designed by R. Woods

Ул. Дунав

0297/0298

20 Искър Искър
Route number
& Destination

Interchange at street level
(10–50-metre walk)

Platform number
(not every stop has one)

1074
Младежки
Театър

0297/0298
Бул. Васил
Лебскм

2168/2169
Ул. Сан
Стефано

Младежки
Театър
1073

Народна
Опера

Искър Искър ㉒

Автостанция Изток ㉒

1700 ㉘④
Су Кл.
Охридски

1903
Ул. Генерал Гурко

Bus route

Пл. Орлов
Мост
1289

Пл. Журналист ②⑫

Ул. Вишнева 1879/1880

1273

㉘④

Семинари Та 1570/1573

Телевиз. Кула

⑱
Пуско Посолство

Sofia International Airport

A Communicarta
Style45 design
© Communicarta Ltd 2006 UDN.1
Map user Ref:WZFG/CS/SOF/2006/21/4

TAXI COMPANIES
OK Supertrans ☎ 973 2121
Taxi S Express ☎ 912 80
Radio CB Taxi ☎ 912 63

kilometre during daytime and 10–15 per cent more at night – but most drivers do not speak English. Taxis can be booked in advance and reception staff at your hotel are usually happy to call one for you and, if necessary, explain to the driver where you want to go.

Getting out of town
You will need to use buses from one of the city's bus stations to reach the excursion destinations in this guide. The Central Bus Station (see page 51) serves Blagoevgrad, while buses to Mount Vitosha depart from the Hladilnika terminus, to the south of the city centre (see page 116). Buses to other destinations south of the city, including Rila Monastery, depart from the Ovcha Kupel terminal (☎ (02) 955 5362), which is 5 km (3 miles) southwest of the centre (see page 118). For travel to Koprivshtitsa, there is a minibus service from the Trafik-Market bus terminal (☎ (02) 981 2979), immediately west of the central railway station.

CAR HIRE
Car hire is hardly worth the trouble of organising when public transport serves the excursion destinations, although a car would be helpful for Rila Monastery. **Avis** (ⓦ www.avis.bg) and **Europcar** (ⓦ www.europcar.bg) have offices at the airport and in the city.

● *The rooftops of Sofia*

Around Sveta Nedelya Square

Sveta Nedelya can be regarded as the centre of the city and a major orientation point when you first start exploring the city. It is a compact area and everywhere can be reached on foot. Vitosha Boulevard, the main shopping street, runs due south from the square, while immediately to the north stands the landmark Balkan Sheraton hotel and the Monument to Holy Wisdom. The main way east from the Sheraton hotel mall leads almost immediately to Nezavisimost Square, also known as the Largo, and this leads to the attractions on the east side of the city. The main street heading north from Sveta Nedelya Square is Maria Luiza Boulevard and it heads towards the bus and railway station. Although Maria Luiza Boulevard accesses some sights, principally the synagogue, it is not long before this street becomes decidedly grotty and the way to the bus and railway stations becomes one of the least attractive thoroughfares in the city.

SIGHTS & ATTRACTIONS

Alexander Batenberg Square

The square near the Party House used to be called the Ninth of September Square, commemorating the date of the Communist takeover in 1944, and it was the focal point for government-related parades until 1989. There used to be a giant mausoleum facing the square, holding the embalmed body of Georgi Dimitrov, the country's first Communist leader. The Bulgarian politburo would stand on the mausoleum to take the salute from goose-stepping troops and the convoys of tanks that rolled by over the cobbles. Dynamite removed the mausoleum in 2000, but ideas for replacing

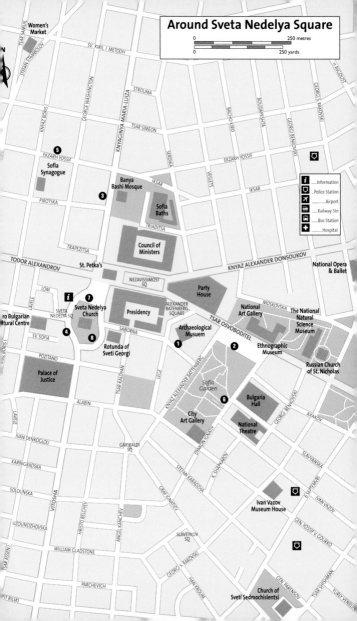

Around Sveta Nedelya Square

| | 0 | 250 metres |
| 0 | | 250 yards |

Women's Market

SV. KIRIL I. METODIY

STEFAN STAMBOLOV

TSAR SAMUIL

GEORGE WASHINGTON

KNYAGINYA MARIA-LUIZA

STROUMA

TSAR SIMEON

SERDICA

BACHO KIRO

BOULDAPESHTA

GEORGI S RAKOVSKI

II AOUST

KNYAZ BORIS

⑤ EKZARH YOSSIF

Sofia
Synagogue

EKZARH YOSSIF

IKSAR

VESLETS

Police Station

PIROTSKA

③ Banya
Bashi Mosque

IKSAR

Information

Police Station

Airport

Railway Stn

Bus Station

Hospital

Sofia
Baths

TRAPEZITSA

TRIADITSA

Council of
Ministers

TODOR ALEXANDROV

St. Petka's

KNYAZ ALEXANDER DONSOUKOV

National Opera
& Ballet

NEZAVISSIMÒST
SQ

LAVELE

LOM

SVETA
NEDELYA
SQ

i

⑦ Sveta Nedelya
Church

Presidency

ALEXANDER
BATENBERG
SQUARE

Party
House

MOSKOVSKA

National
Art Gallery

The National
Natural
Science
Museum

ro Bulgarian
tural Centre

④

⑧

SABORNA

TSAR OSVOBODITEL

SV. SOFIA

Rotunda of
Sveti Georgi

Archaeological
Museum

①

②

Ethnographic
Museum

Russian Church
of St. Nicholas

POZITANO

TSAR KALOMAN

LEGE

KNYAZ ALEXANDER BATTENBERG

Sofia
Garden

⑥

GEORGI BENKOVSKI

Palace of
Justice

Bulgaria
Hall

AXAKOV

ALABIN

City
Art Gallery

National
Theatre

LAVELE

IVAN DENKOGLOU

GARIBALDI
SQ

DIMCON IGNATIV

K. SHEYNAROV

SLAVYANSKA

KARNIGRADSKA

STEFAN KARADJA

SOLOUNSKA

GRAF IGNATIV

6 SEPTEMVRI

IVAN VAZOV

Ivan Vazov
Museum House

GEN. YOSSIF GOURKO

HRISTO BELCHEV

VITOSHA

ANGEL KANCHEV

UZOUNDZHOVSKA

AD ASSEN

WILLIAM GLADSTONE

SLAVEYKOV
SQ

IVAN KROUM

GEORGI S. RAKOVSKI

GEN. PARIÈNOV

TSAR SHISHMAN

YURIY VENILIN

Church of
Sveti Sedmochislentsi

PARCHEVICH

FIT RILSKI

the site with something attractive were not followed through and dull shrubbery covers the ground.

Banya Bashi Mosque

The only city mosque still in use, this takes its name from the nearby mineral baths (*banya bashi* means 'many baths') and dates back to the 16th century. The architect was Hadji Mimar Sinan, the leading Muslim designer of the age and creator of some magnificent edifices outside Bulgaria, but on this project he contented himself with a single large dome and one minaret. Notwithstanding the modesty of the design, the mosque is a singularly attractive addition to the city centre. The mineral baths to the rear of the mosque were built in the early 20th century and rate as one of the architectural highlights of the city, but the building is currently under wraps due to restoration work. When completed – no opening date has yet been announced – the baths will house a new city museum.

ⓐ Maria Luiza Boulevard ⓒ 08.00–17.00. Visitors welcome outside of prayer sessions, especially on Fridays; women should be modestly dressed

The Party House

A short walk around the corner from the Balkan Sheraton on to Nezavisimost Square immediately brings into view the Party House, the large, neoclassical building that was once the headquarters of the country's Communist Party. The building looks powerful, and was even more so when it sported a giant red star on its summit. The star was removed in August 1990 when protestors tried to set it on fire.

ⓐ Nezavisimost Square ⓒ Closed to the public

Pirotska Street and Women's Market

Pirotska Street, one block south of the street where Sofia Synagogue stands, is a pleasant pedestrianised street with small shops occupying old buildings that date back a century or more. At the end of this street, a right turn at the junction where trams cross leads directly to the Women's Market, or Zhenski Pazar, a dense but not claustrophobic open-air bazaar. Farmers sell their fresh produce alongside stalls retailing inexpensive clothing, broomsticks for the

⬥ *National Theatre, Sofia Garden*

home and assorted items. The market has atmosphere and a character that is quite at odds with the air of sophistication being promoted in the rest of the city.

🅐 Pirotska Street and Stefan Stambolov Street 🕒 Women's Market: 08.00–19.00

Sofia Garden

Immediately south of Alexander Batenberg Square, the pretty stretch of green that constitutes Sofia Garden comes into its own with the advent of spring. Local office workers take advantage of the sunshine during their breaks, and chess players settle into studied silence after setting their game clocks. There is more than one place serving drinks and the elegant neoclassical façade of the National Theatre bestows an air of cultural refinement on the park scene.

🅐 South of Alexander Batenberg Square 🕒 24 hours

Sofia Synagogue

Designed and built in the first decade of the 20th century, this elegant and imaginative synagogue is a reminder that one in five of the city's citizens were Jews and respected highly enough to add their cultural contribution to the skyline of the city centre. The Austrian architect designer, Friedrih Gruenager, boldly mixed Moorish and Byzantine features around a large octagonal dome and multiple turrets. The interior is a delightful surprise with art nouveau-style decorations and a giant brass chandelier weighing over 2,000 kg (4,410 lb). Built to house 1,300, attendances now number less than 75; the city's Jews mostly emigrated to Palestine in the late 1940s.

🅐 Ekzarh Yosif Street 🕿 (02) 983 1273 🌐 www.sofiasynagogue.com
🕒 09.30–17.00 Mon–Sat, 09.00–13.00 Sat, closed Sun. Ring the bell for the caretaker; a small charge for depositing any bags

Sveta Nedelya Church

The present church in Sveta Nedelya Square occupies a spot where a succession of churches has stood since medieval times. The location is associated with a Serbian king, Stefan Urish, who ruled Bulgaria in the 14th century and whose bones are preserved in a wooden box to the right of the iconostasis. The church you see today was built in the mid-19th century, and in 1925 it survived a bombing attempt to eliminate the Bulgarian royal family who were in the church attending a funeral. Although the building was badly damaged and over 100 mourners killed, the royals escaped unhurt.

ⓐ Sveta Nedelya Square ⓛ 07.00–19.00. Daily liturgy at 08.30 and 16.00

Sveta Nedelya Square

Named after the church (see above), the square is dominated by the Balkan Sheraton hotel and a 24-m high (79-ft) bronze statue that is supposed to represent Holy Wisdom, the name of the church of Sveta Sofia from which the city supposedly received its name. The statue looks a little daft – a shiny woman holding a bird in one hand and emanating, presumably, a state of holy wisdom – and far less resonant than the huge statue of Lenin that once occupied this spot.

CULTURE

Archaeological Museum

A modest but engaging collection of Thracian, Greek and Roman remains and some medieval artefacts from around the country. The more spectacular exhibits include a Thracian gold burial mask from the 4th century BC that was excavated in 2004. There is also a gravestone from the 6th century BC found at the site of an ancient Greek colony on the Black Sea coast.

Directly across the cobbled street from the museum's entrance are the offices of the Bulgarian president. The entrance is fronted by guards in fancy 19th-century dress, and on the hour they do a quick pirouette routine that is mildly diverting.

ⓐ Lege Street 2 ⓣ (02) 988 2406 ⓦ http://aim.sofianet.net
ⓛ 10.00–1800 Tues–Sun, closed Mon. Admission charge

City Art Gallery

Constantly changing profiles of either contemporary Bulgarian artists or international shows; the information sheets are not in English but with free admission you have nothing to lose by popping in to view the canvases.

ⓐ Gurko Street 1 ⓣ (02) 987 2181 ⓛ 10.00–19.00 Tues–Sat, 11.00–17.00 Sun. Free admission

Ethnographic Museum

Reflecting Bulgarian culture through the centuries, the collections of Balkan arts and crafts that make up this museum are housed in one half of the former royal palace and this explains why features of the building's interior design, the plasterwork especially, is itself an attraction of any visit. The particular theme behind a special exhibition that is showcased while you are in the city may help you to decide whether to make a visit or not. Unlike some of the city museums, the exhibits are all explained in English.

ⓐ Alexander Batenberg Square ⓣ (02) 987 4191 ⓛ 10.00–1800 Tues–Sun, closed Mon. Admission charge

ⓞ *Sveta Nedelya Church*

National Art Gallery

The other half of the former royal palace housing the Ethnographic Museum constitutes the National Art Gallery. The galleries downstairs are devoted to temporary exhibitions of contemporary Bulgarian art, the quality of which varies, while the main galleries use their space to good effect in highlighting the best Bulgarian artists of the past.

ⓐ Alexander Batenberg Square ⓣ (02) 980 3325 ⓛ 10.00–18.00 Tues–Sun, closed Mon. Admission charge

NOT TO BE MISSED IN THE NATIONAL ART GALLERY

Look for the work of Vladimir Dimitrov-Maistora (1882–1960), Bulgaria's greatest artist of the 20th century. His paintings of peasant girls in bucolic settings are strangely alluring because of a near-mystical quality endowed by the colours.

Rotunda of Sveti Georgi

Easy to miss, tucked away behind the Balkan Sheraton hotel, Sofia's oldest church stands in a small courtyard. The red-brick exterior looks uninspiring and only its 4th-century Roman origins would seem to impart significance to the building, but step inside to view some stunning 14th-century frescoes and a depiction of wise men that dates from the 10th and 12th centuries. The church became a mosque during the Ottoman period and the frescoes, painted over, remained hidden until the 20th century.

ⓐ Sveta Nedelya Square ⓛ 08.00–17.00

RETAIL THERAPY

Bulgarski Dyukyan Balkan crockery, embroidered tablecloths, peasant-style copper pots. ❸ Pirotska Street 20 ❶ (02) 980 5491 ❶ 09.30–19.30 Mon–Fri, 10.00–17.00 Sat, closed Sun

Ethnographic Museum Shop Bulgarian kilims at around 150lv per square metre are one of the better buys, but also jewellery, folk artefacts and Bulgarian music. You do not need to visit the museum to check out the shop (which also opens on Mon, when the museum is closed). ❸ Alexander Batenberg Square ❶ (02) 987 4191 ❶ 10.00–18.00

Stenata To find this shop, walk west along Pozitano Street from Sveta Nedelya Square, and Brata Miladinovi Street is on your left. Stenata's stock of hiking, camping and climbing gear is the best in the city. ❸ Brata Miladinovi Street 5 ❶ (02) 980 5491 ❶ www.stenata.com ❶ 10.00–19.00 Mon–Fri, 10.00–18.00 Sat, closed Sun

Tzum Once the consumer showpiece of Communist-era Sofia, now fulfilling a similar function for the post-Communist bourgeoisie of the city: three levels of boutiques, accessories, cafés, cosmetics and foreign newspapers; in the basement, a useful supermarket. ❸ Corner of Maria Luisa Boulevard and Nezavisimost Square ❶ (02) 951 5266 ❶ 10.00–21.00 Mon–Sat, 11.00–20.00 Sun

TAKING A BREAK

Art Museum Café £ ❶ Tucked away at the back of the
Archaeological Museum and attracting a sophisticated-looking set
of customers, this is an ideal spot for coffee and cakes or something
more substantial from a menu of salads and pasta dishes; no
smoking in the downstairs section where the seating rubs
shoulders with ancient gravestones.
🅐 Suborna Street 2 🄵 (02) 988 2610 🄻 09.00–24.00

Bulgaria £ ❷ A very swish café, carpeted, with large glass windows
for street-watching. Have a posh frappé or Viennese coffee with
helpings of tiramisu, strudel or blackberry pie. The truffle and white
chocolate also tempts the palate. 🅐 Tsar Osvoboditel Boulevard 4
🄵 (02) 988 5307 🄻 08.00–22.00

Halite £ ❸ On the top floor of this restored market hall there is a
food court with various food options or, in the basement, a branch
of the always-reliable Trops Kushta. 🅐 Corner of Maria Luiza
Boulevard and Ekzarh Yosif Street 🄻 07.00–24.00

PICNIC PROVISIONS
For picnic food, head for the food court on the top floor of
Halite (see above) or, across the road, the supermarket in the
basement of Tzum (see page 71).

🄿 *The Rotunda of Sveti Georgi, behind the Sheraton*

Happy Bar & Grill £ ❹ You know the interior décor: neon-lit guitars alongside rock and movie posters on the walls, and laminated menus; a bright and cheerful joint for drinks or a quick meal from the menu of grills, chicken and countless salads. Another branch on the east side of the city (see page 84). ➋ Sveta Nedelya Square 4 ❶ (02) 986 1449 ❷ 24 hours

Lion £ ❺ Cross over Ekzrah Yosif Street from the synagogue and Lion restaurant is on the left side of the small street facing you. The lunch menu is in Bulgarian, but the staff will translate dishes like pork steak with cheese or chicken and broccoli. Inexpensive, white tablecloth restaurant and a quiet, calm atmosphere. The à la carte menu (**££**) is in English. ➋ Vashi Nitoi Street 21, off Ekzrah Yosif Street ❶ (02) 983 2826 ❷ 11.00–22.30

Theatre Café £ ❻ Easy to find, facing as it does the stately frontage of the National Theatre in Sofia Garden, this café-bar opens in May and attracts trendy young people at night. ➋ Vasil Levski Street ❶ (02) 980 7865 ❷ 10.00–02.00 (summer only)

AFTER DARK

Restaurants
Balkan ££–£££ ❼ The traditional Bulgarian dishes are your best bet although Mediterranean dishes like chicken with lemon and oregano sauce also feature; elegant setting, international wine list and attentive service. ➋ Balkan Sheraton Hotel, Sveta Nedelya Square ❶ (02) 981 6541

Peter 1 ££–£££ ❽ Just what you expect a Russian restaurant to look like, with portraits of the eponymous tsar and folk dances in frilly costumes at night. Authentic dishes of *blini*, *pelmeni* and *pirogi*. ⓐ Pozitano Street 2 ⓣ (02) 980 6577 ⓛ 12.00–23.00

Nightlife

Buddha Bar The usual oriental paraphernalia and a laid-back atmosphere where the quality of the music is pot luck. ⓐ Lege Street 15A ⓣ (02) 989 5006 ⓛ 24 hours

Toba & Co £ Not the place you are likely to stroll past, Toba & Co needs seeking out at the back of the National Art Gallery. What you eventually find is an odd little joint that livens up when someone is there to spin CDs, but otherwise offers a long list of drinks, including cocktails, and a continental-style décor. Light food also available. ⓐ Moskovska Street 6 ⓣ (02) 989 4996 ⓛ 10.30–03.00

Culture

Bulgaria Hall Home to the Sofia Philharmonic Orchestra, and the acoustics in the two concert halls are first class. ⓐ Aksakov Street ⓣ (02) 987 7656 (ticket office) ⓛ 10.00–13.30, 15.30–18.30

Euro Bulgarian Cultural Centre The most regular events here are film showings (ⓦ www.programata.bg), but other art forms are intermittently scheduled here. ⓐ Boulevard Stamboliyski 17 ⓣ (02) 988 0084 ⓦ www.eubcc.bg

Around Alexander Nevsky Memorial Church

Immediately north of Tsar Osvoboditel Boulevard, just off Vassil Levski, is Alexander Nevsky Memorial Church. Tsar Osvoboditel Boulevard itself leads to Narodno Sabranie Square, another landmark location for orientation purposes, identified by the curving façade of the Radisson SAS hotel. Tsar Shishman Street, the first turning on the left with your back to the entrance of the Radisson, is an important street for accessing bars, restaurants and shops in this area.

SIGHTS & ATTRACTIONS

Alexander Nevsky Memorial Church

Russian architects, principally A N Pomerantsev from St Petersburg, designed this church in the 1880s (building was completed in 1924) with the conscious aim of emulating the architectural glory of Byzantium. They undoubtedly succeeded because the result is a masterpiece that magnificently balances multiple gold-leafed domes to create an aesthetically pleasing structure. It was built to commemorate Russia's costly contribution to Bulgaria's liberation – countless thousands of Russians died fighting in the 1877–8 War of Liberation – and the money was raised by public subscriptions. The name of the church, however, refers to the subject of Eisenstein's famous film, a 13th-century prince who helped preserve Novgorod's independence.

The atmospheric interior is generously decorated with dynamic frescoes illuminated by numerous candles flickering in the darkness and enriched by onyx and alabaster columns adorning the thrones in the iconostasis.

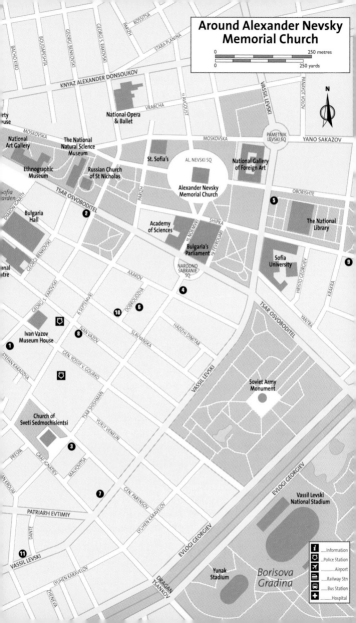

🅐 Alexander Nevsky Square 🕿 (02) 988 1704 🕙 07.00–19.00.
Daily prayers: 08.00 and 17.00. Vigil: 18.30 Sat. Mass: Sun 09.30.
Free admission

Church of Sveti Sedmochislentsi

The bricks and mortar core of this neo-Byzantine pile was originally
part of an Ottoman-era mosque, but the newly liberated Bulgarians
thought it would be more useful as their prison before they gave it
a theological and architectural facelift and transformed it into a
church. Sveti Sedmochislentsi means the 'sacred seven', referring to
the 9th-century saints Cyril and Methodius and their five followers
who, between them, brought Christianity to the pagan Slavs of
Eastern Europe.
🅐 Graf Ignatiev Street 🕿 (02) 987 8023 🕙 07.00–19.00. Daily liturgy:
08.00, 17.00

Graf Ignatiev Street

Graf Ignatiev Street is an extremely busy – by Sofia's standards –
tram-laden thoroughfare that cuts across the city centre from
near Sveta Nedelya Square towards the southeastern outskirts
of the capital. It is named in honour of the Russian count, who
was the grandfather of the novelist Michael Ignatiev. Graf Ignatiev
was instrumental in getting Tsar Alexander III to take on the
Ottoman Empire and thus liberate Bulgaria. Graf Ignatiev Street
goes across Slaveikov Square where there are a number of
bookshops and open-air bookstalls, before it becomes part of
the city's main fruit and vegetable market (🕙 09.30–17.00). At
the point where Graf Ignatiev Street meets Tsar Shishman Street,
which runs northeast up to the Radisson hotel, stands the church
of Sveti Sedmochislentsi.

Narodno Sabranie Square

Tsar Osvoboditel Boulevard connects Sveta Nedelya Square in the west of the city with Narodno Sabranie Square (National Assembly Square) in the east. This large cobbled area is defined on its north side by the country's parliament building and, facing it on the south side in front of the Radisson hotel, a 14-m (46-ft) monument depicting Tsar Alexander II of Russia on horseback. The tsar is honoured because it was his declaration of war on the Ottoman Empire that led to Bulgarian independence. Those who actually did the fighting are represented in the reliefs around the pedestal.

Russian Church of St Nicholas

The Russian theme continues with this highly photogenic and spirited creation gracing Tsar Osvoboditel Boulevard. The green steeple and the perfectly proportioned golden onion domes create an effervescence that is cheerfully at odds with the dour concrete that makes up so many of the buildings on this thoroughfare. The church was built in the early 20th century to serve the city's Russian elite and would not look out of place in the Kremlin. The interior is dark and mysterious, filled with the scent of burning candles and incense.

ⓐ Tsar Osvoboditel Boulevard 3 ⓣ (02) 986 2715 ⓛ 08.30–18.30. Free admission

CULTURE

Crypt of Alexander Nevsky Memorial Church

The unrivalled collection of icons in the church's crypt is from all parts of the country, a result of scouring obscure churches and isolated monasteries, and covering almost a millennium in time.

The majority of icons date from the last two centuries; the rarest are unique examples of medieval iconography; and a common pictorial theme is of the warrior saints George and Demetrius slaying dragons – a coded representation of the struggle against Ottoman oppression.

🅐 Entrance to the left of the church doors in Alexander Nevsky Square 🕒 10.30–17.30 Wed–Mon, closed Tues. Admission charge

Ivan Vazov Museum House

Ivan Vazov (1850–1922) is regarded as the country's greatest writer, certainly the most revered, and his novel *Under the Yoke*, set in a small town at the time of the uprising against Ottoman rule in 1876, is the one most Bulgarians are likely to be familiar with. He lived in this house for the last 25 years of his life, and his abode and its contents have been carefully preserved, making it a fairly unique period piece. Although all the information captions are in Bulgarian only, there is a tangible sense of history about the place that takes you back over a century to another age. The stuffed dog in a room upstairs was Vazov's pet until run over by a tram in the street outside.

🅐 Ivan Vazov Street 10 ☎ (02) 988 1270 🕒 13.00–17.00 Tues–Thur, 11.00–17.00 Fri & Sat, closed Mon & Sun. Admission charge

National Gallery of Foreign Art

Eclectic is the best way to describe what is on show, and the chances are that you will find something surprising and rewarding. The Asian art from Burma and Japan makes up the most gratifying exhibits for many visitors. Minor European art includes a Picasso

🅞 *Golden domes of the Russian Church*

lithograph, drawings by Delacroix and Renoir, and a bewitching piece by Franz von Stick. The basement contains a 4th-century Roman tomb.

ⓐ Alexander Nevsky Square 1 ⓣ (02) 988 4922 ⓦ www.ngfa.icb.bg
ⓛ 11.00–18.00 Wed–Mon, closed Tues. Admission charge, but free on Mon

RETAIL THERAPY

Alexander Nevsky Square Market A not-to-be-missed flea market selling World War II and Communist-era memorabilia, stamps, postcards, coins, medals and assorted bric-a-brac. Very little schlock apart from the cheaply lacquered Russian dolls and the array of reproduction icons. Cross the square to the eastern side for women selling embroidered lace, cardigans and tablecloths.

ⓐ From the corner of Alexander Nevsky Square and 11 August Street
ⓛ 09.00–18.00

Art Gallery Paris Art Gallery Paris is a small, owner-run gallery selling original work by a new generation of unknown Bulgarian

THE BEST MARKET IN SOFIA

For antiques of the kind that will fit easily into your luggage there is nowhere more tempting than the market immediately north of the Alexander Nevsky Memorial Church. World War II items range from German helmets and medals to submarine stop-watches, and one trader does a nice line in Soviet-era hip flasks carrying KGB insignia (or are these just clever fakes?).

artists specialising in figurative and expressive art. Parizh Street runs along the west side of Alexander Nevsky Memorial Church and the shop is near the National Opera House.

ⓐ Parizh Street 8 ⓣ (02) 980 8093 ⓦ www.gallery-paris.com
ⓛ 11.00–19.00 Mon–Fri, closed Sat & Sun

Cheers Three outlets in this part of the city with good selections of Bulgarian wines and spirits. ⓐ Vasil Levski Boulevard 59
ⓣ (02) 987 1272 ⓐ Tsar Osvoboditel Boulevard 14 ⓣ (02) 986 1856
ⓐ G.S. Rakovski Street 116 ⓣ (02) 981 2729 ⓛ 09.00–22.00 Mon–Sat, 10.00–21.00 Sun

Gaya Gallery Paintings, ceramics and mobiles by young artists selling their work for the first time. The shop next door is also worth a visit for its home-made jewellery. Krakra Street is around the corner from the Crystal Palace hotel. ⓐ Krakra Street 19 ⓣ (02) 943 3591 ⓛ 11.00–19.00 Mon–Fri, 11.00–17.00 Sat, closed Sun

Mizella Bratova Mizella Bratova, the designer who makes the clothes you see in this one-off boutique, works with linen and silk to produce trousers, jackets and suits for women and some lovely tops using Thai silk. One of the more original designers in Sofia.
ⓐ Tsar Shishman Street 4 ⓣ (02) 980 7156 ⓛ 10.30–20.00 Mon–Fri, 10.30–18.00 Sat, closed Sun

Noe Art Gallery Original Bulgarian art work – paintings, wood and bronze carvings – of some quality. You could engage in a little gentle bargaining but prices are reasonable. ⓐ Parizh Street 6
ⓣ (02) 980 6941 ⓦ www.gallerynoe.com ⓛ 12.00–18.30 Mon–Fri, closed Sat & Sun

Puta Gallery This gallery, around the corner from Art Gallery Paris, has some paintings for sale but you are also likely to find sculptures and other art forms. Well worth a visit because the stock varies and something very interesting could turn up. 🚇 Vrabcha Street 14 ☎ 0887 769392 🕐 11.00–19.00 Mon–Fri, 11.00–17.00 Sat, closed Sun

Vlaga Blaggoeva A couple of doors up from the Cheers wine shop (see page 83), this is one of a number of single-proprietor boutiques along this street. The limited stock varies from week to week so if you like something, buy it. Further along Vasil Levski Boulevard, between this shop and the Mahaloto restaurant (see page 86), there is a courtyard with half a dozen or more such tiny shops. Little or no English is spoken so just point, smile and try it on. 🚇 Vasil Levski Boulevard 59 ☎ (02) 987 1267 🕐 10.00–22.00

TAKING A BREAK

Happy Bar & Grill £ ❶ The same menu as in the Sveta Nedelya Square branch (see page 74) and its popularity can make the tables inside seem crowded and cramped; it's more relaxing outside where a Parisian-style pavement-café scene prevails. 🚇 G.S. Rakovski Boulevard 145 ☎ (02) 980 7353 🕐 24 hours

Onda £ ❷ A very Western-style joint where latte-sipping café habitués will feel at home. Cookies, muffins and sandwiches are on the menu and, upstairs, superb views of the Russian Church of St Nicholas which is directly across the street. Wireless internet connection is available here. 🚇 Tsar Osvoboditel Boulevard 8A ☎ (02) 986 5643 🕐 07.00–21.00

Mamma Mia £–££ ❸ Cheap and cheerful pasta and pizza restaurant with upstairs tables on a terrace; the tables on your left as you enter the courtyard belong to the cosy Mediterrani bar which is under its own management. ⓐ Tsar Shishman Street 39 ❶ (02) 986 8921 ❻ 11.00–01.00

Flannagans £–£££ ❹ Come here on Sunday for a long brunch (❻ 12.30–16.00) featuring Western, Indian, Italian and Middle Eastern edibles, or drop in anytime for a cold beer and pub food. ⓐ Radisson SAS Hotel, Narodno Sabranie Square 4 ❶ (02) 993 4740 ❻ 12.00–01.00

⬤ Designer linen and silk at Mizella Bratova

AFTER DARK

Restaurants

Bibliotekata £–££ ❺ Nothing academic about this combined sushi bar, set apart in a traditional Japanese setting, and adjoining live-music club in a basement of the National Library. Over a dozen choices of sushi and plenty of main dishes along the lines of scallop with cream, spicy sauce, teriyaki chicken, beef teppanyaki and a dessert of ice cream tempura! ❷ Vasil Levski Boulevard 88 ❶ (02) 943 3978 ❸ Sushi bar: 12.00–24.00. Club: 21.30–04.00

Egur, Egur ££ ❻ Armenian restaurant where the wallpaper, varnished wood flooring and (unplayed) piano create a homely and comfortable mood. Appetising starters like the Armenian sausages or *shtoratz* (fried aubergine rolls), followed by mostly meat-based dishes like *massis* (chicken stuffed with salmon and spinach) with a choice of tasty garnishes. ❷ Dobrudzha Street 10 ❶ (02) 989 3383 ❸ 11.30–24.00

Mahaloto ££ ❼ Mahaloto (Bulgarian for 'pendulum') is rather special because it creates an intimate restaurant atmosphere without sacrificing the need for carefully prepared meals and good service. There are familiar Bulgarian dishes on the menu but the more Western dishes are equally good – a rare achievement – and there is a decent wine list (though no cocktails). A brick cellar setting but tables also outside in the summer. ❷ Vasil Levski Boulevard 51 ❶ 0887 617 972 ❸ 11.00–24.00

Checkpoint Charly £££ ❽ The name refers to the crossing point on the Berlin Wall, and the Cold War theme is playfully persistent in this stylish restaurant – the placemats reproduce Bulgaria's old Communist newspaper. At weekends a live jazz band performs. The food is international and receives good reviews. A night here could extend well into the next morning if followed up by a visit next door to My Mojito (see page 88). ⓐ Ivan Vazov Street 12 ⓣ (02) 988 0370 ⓛ 19.00–02.00 Mon–Fri, 10.00–02.00 Sat & Sun

Crystal Palace Restaurant £££ ⓽ Sedate and civilised: candles on the table, touches of greenery, cocktails and foie gras. The menu is strong on seafood but there are meat dishes as well. Standards are high and the night can be extended into the early hours with a three-minute walk up the street to O! Shipka (see page 114) for drinks and conviviality. ⓐ Crystal Palace Hotel, Shipka Street 14 ⓣ (02) 948 9488 ⓛ 18.30–22.00

Krim £££ ⓾ The most stately of Sofia's restaurants, set in and outside a 19th-century grand house, and one of the few that has survived from the Communist era. Bulgarian, Russian and fish dishes. ⓐ Slavyanska Street 17 ⓣ (02) 988 6950 ⓛ 12.00–24.00

Uno Enoteca £££ ⑪ One of Sofia's very best and most European restaurants. Come here for an atmosphere of subdued elegance. Starters include Parma ham with melon, foie gras or a Caesar salad, and the choice of dishes will satisfy carnivores and vegetarians. An exemplary wine list and impeccable service. ⓐ Vasil Levski Boulevard 45 ⓣ (02) 981 4372 ⓛ 12.00–24.00

Nightlife
Blaze A neat and unpretentiously stylish bar on two levels where you can listen to some excellent sounds through the speakers and

mingle with the budding intelligentsia from the nearby university.
ⓐ Slavanska Street 36 ⓣ (02) 980 5756 ⓛ 09.00–15.00

Bluzz & Rock £ Never mind the spelling, enjoy the live rock 'n' roll,
blues or jazz that kicks off on a Wednesday to Saturday night at
22.00; or take the steps down into this amiable pub-restaurant any
day or night for drinks – wine by the glass or bottle, draught and
bottled beers – and a pizza. ⓐ G.S. Rakovski Boulevard 112 ⓣ (02) 988
3898 ⓛ 11.00–02.00

My Mojito Dark and cosy club with two DJs spinning soft and
soothing sounds in separate rooms – a relaxed watering hole for
Sofia's sophisticated young ones; a good list of cocktails and a
sociable atmosphere. ⓐ Ivan Vazov Street 14 ⓣ (02) 988 8978
ⓛ 21.00–05.00

Piano Bar Jack A basement bar beneath the Bulgarian army theatre
where a grand piano is brought into play at night and music belted
out until the early hours. Sociable and stylish and a great place to
drop into after dinner. ⓐ G.S. Rakovski Street 98 ⓣ (02) 987 9198
ⓛ 20.00–04.00

Culture
National Opera House Built in 1909 and seating 1,200, this is the
venue for operas and ballets. Some operas are sung in Bulgarian and
some in Italian, so check beforehand.
ⓐ Vrabcha Street 1 ⓣ Ticket office (02) 981 1549 ⓛ 08.30–19.30

ⓓ *The lively Piano Bar Jack*

JACK

PIANO

BAR

Around Vitosha Boulevard

Vitosha Boulevard begins at the southern side of Sveta Nedelya Square and stretches south in a long straight line as if heading directly for Mount Vitosha, which looms attractively in the distance. Once filled with traffic, Vitosha Boulevard is now barred to vehicles except for the clunking trams that trundle up and down, lending a pleasantly old-fashioned feel to the broad street. The mostly featureless buildings that line each side of the boulevard have been converted at street level into upmarket shops, and Vitosha Boulevard is now the premier shopping area for city residents; the all-too-familiar brand names and logos help to make it the most European-looking part of Sofia. The triumph of consumerism in this area leaves little space for cultural attractions, although the boulevard does lead to the National Palace of Culture and a large green area devoted to rest and relaxation.

SIGHTS & ATTRACTIONS

National Palace of Culture

Usually referred to as NDK, this monstrous edifice was constructed in 1981 to celebrate the country's 13th centennial, although it now seems only to celebrate the worst excesses of unimaginative architects who worked for the government in the Communist era. It houses concert halls, exhibition space, shops, offices and, in the basement area, the city's main cinema complex. See the 'After dark' section (page 101) for information on cultural performances and the cinema.

ⓐ Bulgaria Square 1 ☎ (02) 916 6830 ⏰ 09.00–23.00

Palace of Justice

The massive, colonnaded building that dominates the start of Vitosha Boulevard was once the Palace of Justice, but the two lions that adorn its façade now guard an empty building. It housed the National History Museum (see page 108) until 2000 and now no one seems to know what to do with the available space – one of the most impressive-looking buildings in the city – so expect anything from a fast-food outlet to a cultural institute.

❷ Vitosha Boulevard 1 🕐 Closed to the public

The Thirteen Hundred Years Monument

As you enter Yuzhen Park at the junction of Vitosha Boulevard and Patriarh Evtimii Boulevard, look for what resembles a grotesquely vandalised structure. This hideous metal agglomeration is the Thirteen Hundred Years Monument, built in 1981 to mark the anniversary of AD 681 when Khan Asparuh led the Bulgars into what is now Bulgaria. What you see is a strong contender for the ugliest example of Soviet-era public art anywhere in the world.

❷ Northern end of Yuzhen Park

Yuzhen Park

This is the most popular park for the city's youth, and every evening and weekend the place is like a magnet for teenagers who hang out here with their skateboards or simply sit and dangle their legs over the concrete parapets – the pedestrian bridge that leads from behind the NDK towards the Hilton Hotel is a favourite spot for romantically inclined couples. There are kiosks selling candyfloss and drinks, and just before the pedestrian bridge a bar with outdoor aluminium seating where a drink and a snack can be enjoyed in the daytime or at night. It is only on the other side of the Hilton that actual greenery makes an appearance and even then it has a fairly unkempt appearance that tends to put you off wandering through it. ❷ Between Vitosha Boulevard and Fritjof Nansen, beginning where Vitosha Boulevard meets Patriarh Evtimii Boulevard

RETAIL THERAPY

Ambitsia Fashion House This is the new-age Sofia: a fashion house, the work of three designers, dedicated to the assertion of fashion statements for the working woman. The website explains the philosophy and provides examples of the clothes. ❷ Knyaz Boris Street 72 ❶ (02) 981 8165 ❿ www.ambitsia.com ❶ 10.00–19.00 Mon–Fri, 11.30–17.00 Sat, closed Sun

Art Alley Gallery Bulgarian and international art work for sale, based around exhibitions that tend to change every month or so, with any necessary packing arranged by the shop. From Vitosha Boulevard, turn into William Gladstone Street and cross two blocks; the shop is on your right just after crossing Angel Kanchev Street at the end of the second block. ❷ William Gladstone Street 51A ❶ (02) 986 7363 ❶ 10.00–20.00

Bitsiani A fashion store with a reasonably large stock of snazzy jackets, shirts and ties. Shoes are on the level above and sportswear is downstairs. There is also a branch at Pirotska Street 18 and another one at Graf Ignatiev Street 23. ❷ Vitosha Boulevard 32 ❶ (02) 989 7409 ❶ 10.00–20.00 Mon–Sat, 11.00–19.00 Sun

Gallery Miniature To find this wonderful little gallery, walk down Vitosha Boulevard from Sveta Nedelya Church and take the fourth

turning on the right, Karnigradska Street, and turn left off it after passing J.J. Murphy's pub. This brings you on to Kniaz Boris Street and the gallery is down here on the right side. Nikola Litchkov is the sculptor and his son Milen the graphic artist, and between them they produce some excellent work. The miniatures in oils and watercolour, depicting scenes of country life and moments from traditional Bulgarian folk tales, are priced between 60lv and 150lv while the sculptures start at around 300lv and go up to 1,000lv.
📍 Kniaz Boris I Street 55 ☎ (02) 986 5439 🕐 10.00–18.00

Knigomania The best bookshop for English-language material, including hiking maps of Mount Vitosha. 📍 Boulevard Vitosha 9
☎ (02) 987 1859 🌐 www.knigomania.com 🕐 Mon–Fri 09.30–19.30, 10.00–18.00 Sat & Sun

Pamela Megan This expensive boutique is at the bottom end of Vitosha Boulevard, just past the junction with Patriarh Evtimii Boulevard and the entrance to Yuzhen Park. Upmarket designs from Italy, France and Greece for fashion-conscious women. There are two other shops close by on the same stretch of street, Paola Apsi and Victor Uomo, under the same management and retailing similar gear. 📍 Vitosha Boulevard 86 ☎ (02) 952 6812 🕐 10.00–20.00 Mon–Fri, 10.30–19.30 Sat, closed Sun

Tom Tailor German designs in smart casual gear in one of the outlets in the Alexander building; mostly for men but a small selection for women as well. 📍 Vitosha Boulevard 21 ☎ (02) 981 5051
🕐 10.00–20.30

▶ *The Thirteen Hundred Years Monument*

Visages A small shop stocking jewellery imported from Turkey. Located on the left side of Neofit Rilski Street if turning into the street when walking down Vitosha Boulevard from Sveta Nedelya Church. ⓐ Neofit Rilski Street 41 ⓣ (02) 981 4536 ⓛ 09.00–20.00 Mon–Fri, 09.00–18.00 Sat, closed Sun

TAKING A BREAK

Buia Pocure £ ❶ Look for a blue plaque on the wall outside, and if you find yourself passing the Niky hotel you have missed it. Tucked away in a quiet courtyard, this is a neat little hideaway from the hubbub of Vitosha Boulevard. Cakes and chocolate truffles, coffees and a tempting choice of croissants, including ones stuffed with mozzarella and tomato or Brie and broccoli. Cocktails and fruit drinks and outdoor tables in the shade. ⓐ Neofit Rilski Street 8 ⓣ (02) 954 3072 ⓛ 09.00–21.00

Dream House £ ❷ Look for a sign for the entrance to the Internet Hostel, open the white door on the left and walk up the staircase to reach this vegetarian restaurant. Snack on starters like vegetable sushi in a spicy sauce with an avocado salad or make a meal of it with tofu and rice in sweet and sour sauce, or grilled courgette and tahini sauce. An eatery during the day but more restaurant-like at night; a buffet all day Sunday. Good drinks list. ⓐ Alabin Street 50A ⓣ (02) 980 8163 ⓛ 11.30–22.00

Pizza Palace £ ❸ For an inexpensive eatery open around the clock, it is hard to beat Pizza Palace. There are regular meat dishes on the menu but city residents come here for the piping hot and very affordable pizzas. At lunchtimes the restaurant can become quite full, inside and out, but it is ideal for an early or late meal during the day. ⓐ Vitosha Boulevard 34 ⓣ (02) 986 7187 ⓛ 24 hours

Pizza Troll £ ❹ With the proviso that the pizzas are not the best in Sofia – those at Pizza Palace, further down on the other side of the street, are far better – the service is fast and efficient, and if you want a quick bite on the way to somewhere else Pizza Troll does the business. ⓐ Vitosha Boulevard 8 ⓣ (02) 988 7654 ⓛ 24 hours

AFTER DARK

Restaurants
Dani's £ ❺ Excellent little deli-café, ideal for a lunch break on a warm day when the home-made lemonade goes down a treat with a salad, soup and sandwich. ⓐ Angel Kanchev 12 ⓣ (02) 980 4548 ⓛ 10.00–22.00

J.J. Murphy's £ ❻ All too familiar Irish-theme pub in some respects, but reassuring when it comes to delivering a decent pint of Murphy's and recognisable dishes like shepherd's pie. This is also the best place to be sure of catching a satellite-transmitted soccer match; live music at weekends. ⓐ Karnigradska Street 6 ⓣ (02) 980 2870 ⓛ 12.00–00.30

Niky £–££ ❼ The garden setting and the parrots make you forget this is a hotel-restaurant, and the wood-burning fireplace creates a cosy atmosphere in cold weather. A wide-ranging menu, with a small vegetarian selection, and a good choice of drinks. ⓐ Niky Hotel, Neofit Rilski Street 16 ⓣ (02) 851 1915 ⓛ 11.00–23.00

Monastirska Magernitsa ££   A contender for that last night in the city when you want a leisurely dining experience and a reminder that you are well and truly in the Balkans. The setting is perfect – a 19th-century house decorated in traditional Bulgarian style – for a menu of time-honoured dishes from the country's many monasteries. ⓐ Han Asparuh Street 67 ⓣ (02) 980 3883 ⓛ 11.00–02.00

Peter 1 ££   Peter I was one of the great Russian tsars and there is no mistaking the Russian nature of this restaurant. The generously sized cellar-like setting with brick arches is brought to life by the deep-red colour theme. The sturgeon or caviar are the most tempting starters – not least because of the prices – followed by classic dishes like stroganoff or *basturma* (marinated veal). A band plays Russian music nightly. ⓐ Pozitano Street 2 ⓣ (02) 980 6577 ⓛ 12.00–24.00

Pri Yafata ££   A good place to start satisfying your curiosity about Bulgarian cuisine because the grilled meats and salads are authentic national favourites. The décor looks kitschy but is actually genuine. ⓐ Solunska Street 28 ⓣ (02) 980 1727 ⓛ 10.00–01.00

Upstairs ££   Fashionable diner with metal chairs on a narrow balcony overlooking Sofia's main drag, and tables and sofas in the arty interior. You can turn up for just drinks and enjoy the scene or tuck into the salads, pasta or dishes like chicken satay and pineapple. Coffees include a Drambuie-topped 'Prince Charles' ('for refined gentlemen') and plenty of cocktails. ⓐ Vitosha Boulevard 18 ⓣ (02) 989 9696 ⓛ 09.00–02.00 Mon–Fri, 10.00–02.00 Sat & Sun

Da Vidi £££   The minimalist style and floor-to-ceiling windows may be a familiar format in other European cities, but this is hip stuff for Sofia and makes for an agreeable night out. The continental-style food is well-prepared with excellent fish dishes,

◔ *Giant lion guarding the Palace of Justice*

and the wine list goes well beyond the national confines.

ⓐ Han Asparuh Street 36 **ⓣ** (02) 980 6746 **ⓛ** 11.00–22.00 Mon–Sat, 18.00–22.00 Sun

Nightlife

Escape Escape is Sofia's number-one nightclub where techno and house music is belted out from the top-notch sound system. High-flying DJ acts are part of the attraction (Mark Spoon, Déjà Vu, Super

ⓐ *National Palace of Culture (NDK)*

Funk...), and the website gives you a good idea of what to expect. Sophisticated in many respects but also boasting the fact that Jean-Claude Van Damme turned up here one night.
ⓐ Angel Kanchev 1 ⓣ 0885 111 215 ⓦ www.clubescapebg.com

Funky Town This neon-lit bar, at the bottom end of Vitosha Boulevard, describes itself as being located in downtown Sofia – perhaps more of an aspiration than a reality – but, notwithstanding, it is an amiable joint where you could chill out when the music is not too loud. ⓐ Han Asparuh Street 65A ⓣ (02) 980 5496
ⓛ 12.00–03.00

Sheherezada OK, so this is a place where Bulgarian dancers in frilly dresses cavort to the sounds of folksy music and the waiters are dressed in hyper-Balkan costumes, but it is not as naff as it seems, and everyone works hard to keep a party mood going through the night. ⓐ Vitosha Boulevard 1A ⓣ (02) 988 8240
ⓛ 21.00–06.00. Small admission charge

Culture
National Palace of Culture With a main hall seating nearly 4,000 and a number of smaller halls and exhibition spaces, this is not surprisingly the main venue for high-profile cultural events. Movie premieres, pop concerts and major concerts of classical music take place in the main hall, while the other two halls are given over to chamber music and classical recitals. The large public spaces around the various foyers often host art exhibitions so see what is on at the time of your visit. Check out ⓦ www.programata.bg for current listings. ⓐ Bulgaria Square 1 ⓣ Ticket office (02) 916 6369
ⓛ Mon–Sat 09.00–19.00, closed Sun

United New Cinema This is the most accessible cinema complex in
the city, reached by walking down Boulevard Vitosha and through
the park, or by tram from the end of Alabin Street near Sveta
Nedelya Square. There are eight screens, showing mostly
Hollywood blockbusters, and tickets can be booked in advance
(advisable at weekends). Weekly programmes are listed on
ⓦ www.programata.bg and in the weekly *Sofia Echo*. ⓐ Basement
area of National Palace of Culture ⓣ (02) 951 5101 ⓛ 11.00–23.00
Ⓝ Tram: No 9

SITE INTERNET
The Site Internet Café, halfway down Vitosha Boulevard,
opposite Pizza Palace (see page 96), is the best place in the city
to connect to the web. You can also download your digital
photographs and use Skype phones here.
ⓐ Vitosha Boulevard 45 ⓣ (02) 986 0896 ⓛ 24 hours

● *Sveta Sofia statue at the end of Vitosha Boulevard*

Outside the centre

Sofia's most significant cultural attractions, the medieval frescoes at Boyana Church and the National History Museum, are located 8 km (5 miles) southwest of the city centre in the affluent suburb of Boyana. It is a 20-minute ride by taxi and, although it takes over an hour by public transport, the bus journey is straightforward enough. Begin by catching tram No 9 on Alabin Street, a five-minute walk away from Sveta Nedelya Square, to its terminus at Hladilnika. From here, it takes half a minute to walk through the tiny market of wooden stalls – just follow fellow passengers – to the street with a number of bus stops. Turn left and walk 300 m (330 yds) past the bus stops to an open area with more bus stops, and look for the one indicating bus No 64, which goes past Boyana Church. Bus No 63 from Toteben Boulevard passes the National History Museum, or catch trolleybus No 2 from outside Sofia University to its terminus and then walk up to and cross the main street, turn left and walk 200 m (219 yds) for an entrance road to the museum.

The other sights and attractions outside the centre are reachable on foot or by a short taxi ride.

SIGHTS & ATTRACTIONS

Borisova Gradina

From the Soviet Army Monument, it is a minute's walk to the entrance of the city's most spacious and attractive park and two stadia. Renamed Borisova Gradina (Boris Garden) after 1989, it is still known as Freedom Park – a name associated with the Communist era and discarded for this reason. Developed and perfected by three successive gardeners, the park is large enough never to feel

crowded, and joggers have the footpaths to themselves early in the morning. Ideal for picnics on a warm day.

ⓐ South of Orlov Most ⏱ 24 hours. Free admission

The Soviet Army Monument

From Narodno Sabraine Square, Tsar Osvoboditel Boulevard heads towards Orlov Most (Eagle's Bridge), which crosses the puny River Perlovska. The bridge marks the spot where returning Bulgarian prisoners of war, released from Ottoman prisons after liberation in 1878, were greeted rapturously by their fellow citizens. The prisoners were christened the eagles, hence the creatures adorning the bridge on each side.

Before reaching the bridge, you will see the Soviet Army Monument, erected in 1944 to acknowledge the liberation of the country from Nazi submission. Although it is reviled by some Bulgarians because of the odious associations with the Soviet era that followed the end of World War II, it is a superb example of monumental sculpture and the best piece of public art in the city. Friezes around the base, depicting scenes of men and women fighting, are remarkably dynamic and convey a dramatic sense of movement. Confronting a brave new future, 34 m (111¹/₂ ft) above these scenes, a Red Army soldier stands in solidarity with a worker and a peasant female with her child. Skateboarders practise their skills around the monument, seemingly oblivious to their own history.

ⓐ Tsar Osvoboditel Boulevard near Orlov Most ⏱ 24 hours

CULTURE

Boyana Church

The work of anonymous 13th-century artists, the church frescoes are

Bulgaria's most important contribution to medieval European culture – not least because they are so well preserved and complete – and careful restoration work shows just how astonishing the artists' achievement was. Art historians compare their mastery of pictorial realism, use of the vernacular and mature awareness of colour to the achievement of Giotto (who was not even born when work began on these frescoes), founder of the Florentine school of painting and harbinger of the Italian Renaissance. How influential the Boyana artists were in the development of Western European painting is the subject of debate, though there is no disputing their effect on mural painting in Russia and Eastern Europe. Although the frescoes pay homage to the canon of medieval icon painting and the traditions of Byzantine art, there is no mistaking the innovatory display of individuality and celebration of ordinary life in the more than 240 figures that populate the frescoes.

Visitor numbers and their time inside the church are strictly limited, and to study the frescoes in detail you will need to visit the nearby church museum where reproductions are on display.

ⓐ Boyansko Ezero Street, Boyana ❶ (02) 959 0939
ⓦ www.boyanachurch.org ❶ 09.00–17.00. Admission charge

PATRON OF THE ARTS

In 1259, Sevastocrator Kaloyan expanded the church at Boyana and commissioned a group of artists – their names lost to posterity – to illuminate the interior with frescoes. One of the finest paintings you will see in Boyana depicts Kaloyan in the contemporary dress of nobles holding a model of the church in his hands alongside his wife Desislava.

National History Museum

The city and the country's most prestigious museum, once located in the heart of the city, was moved to the suburb of Boyana to make use of a grand palatial building once used by the Communist government. It makes sense, perhaps, to pay a visit if travelling to Boyana Church but, at least for the next couple of years, it is debatable if a dedicated journey just to see the museum is worthwhile. The prime reason for this is that the most outstanding collection, the treasures of ancient Thrace, is travelling to France, Switzerland and Japan and will not be on show in the museum. Even some of the medieval artefacts on display are replicas of material kept elsewhere in the country, and little of the labelling is in English. What you will see is an engaging ethnographic exhibition on the top floor, assorted artefacts from the ancient times and the Middle Ages, and a collection of frescoes from monasteries around the country.

ⓐ Vitoshko Lale 16, Boyana ① (02) 955 42 80
ⓦ www.historymuseum.org ① 09.30–18.00 (Apr–Oct); 09.00–17.30 (Nov–Mar), closed on New Year's Day and 24 & 25 Dec. Admission charge and additional charge for use of a camera

National Military History Museum

The paraphernalia in the cabinets inside the museum – uniforms, weapons and the like – will tend to appeal only to military buffs, but the hardware on show outside is the real draw. There are MiG jet fighters, missile launchers and SS23 missiles from the Soviet era alongside the phenomenally versatile Russian T34 tank that played a crucial role in the defeat of German forces by the USSR.

▶ *Enormous keys help protect the Boyana Church frescoes*

📍 Cherkovna Street 92 📞 (02) 946 1806 🕐 10.00–18.00 Wed–Sun, closed Mon & Tues

RETAIL THERAPY

Traditzia A worthy, EU-funded project supporting ethnic minorities and people with disabilities in Bulgaria by selling their handicrafts: ceramics, hand-made stationery, glassware, kilims and linen. The shop is on the south side of Vasil Levski Boulevard, close to the junction with 6 September Street. 📍 Vasil Levski Boulevard 36 📞 (02) 981 7765 🌐 www.traditzia.bg 🕐 11.00–19.00 Tues–Sat, closed Mon

TAKING A BREAK

There is a small café inside the **National History Museum**, but nothing in the immediate vicinity of Boyana Church, and so it is advisable to either bring picnic food or time your visit between meal times.

Artists Bar £ ❶ A few mediocre paintings on easels rather lamely justify the name of this bar in the Hilton Hotel, but this does not detract from its value as a sedate watering hole before or after watching a movie below the National Palace of Culture (NDK) or in the City Centre Sofia complex. Cocktails and live piano music from 18.00–20.00 nightly and on Wed and Thurs live jazz from 22.00. Food too: salads and snacks like chicken satay, panini and sandwiches, and meals like chilli con carne and lamb shashlik. 📍 Hilton Hotel, Bulgaria Boulevard 1 📞 (02) 933 5050 🕐 08.00–02.00

Hedena £ ❷ Located between the Hilton Hotel and the City Centre Sofia shopping mall and cinema, but on the other side of the street,

Hedena serves gourmet coffees and milkshakes at pavement tables.
ⓐ Fritof Nansen 30 ⓣ (02) 969 2450 ⓛ 09.30–22.00

O! Shipka £ ❸ Well worth seeking out for an inexpensive but tasty pizza, salad or Mexican-style dish. Tables inside, where sociability raises the noise level, or a pleasant garden setting where peace and quiet can be enjoyed and a glass of wine or two sipped contentedly. A nightclub of the same name is downstairs (see page 114).
ⓐ Shipka Street 11 ⓣ (02) 944 9388 ⓛ 12.00–24.00

AFTER DARK

Restaurants
Arkadia ££ ❹ Hidden away down a quiet street – walking down Sveti Naum from the Hilton end, take the second left, but if you reach the Lotenetz Hotel you have gone past the turning – this restaurant and bar is not known to many visitors and it makes for a perfect getaway and a quiet meal. The menu features a variety of starters, more than half a dozen vegetarian dishes, fondue (Bulgarian style) and all sorts of meats. Eat inside, downstairs (where there is a snooker table and dartboard) or outside. A good list of Bulgarian wines. ⓐ Krum Popov Street 64 ⓣ (02) 865 8484 ⓛ 11.00–02.00

Hadzhidraganovite Kashti ££–£££ ❺ There are not many good reasons for wandering up to this part of town, between Sveta Nedlya Square and the bus and railway stations, but this traditional Bulgarian restaurant is one. There are four themed rooms, each reflecting the ethnography of a different region of the country, and folk musicians work their way around them in the course of the

STUDENTSKI GRAD

Studentski Grad, 'student city', is a suburb 7 km (4⅓ miles) southeast of the city centre and home to 10,000 bright young people intent on having a good time when not inside a lecture theatre. There are countless bars and pubs, and the neighbourhood can be reached by taking a bus from Shipka Street to the end of the line. You will need a taxi to get back to town but they are easy to find around the bars. ⓐ Bus: No 280

evening. A long menu with most of the national favourites – the oven-cooked lamb can be vouched for although the jury is out on the 'stuffed hen in a clay egg'. ⓐ Kozloduy Street 75 ⓣ (02) 931 31 48 ⓦ www.kashtite.com ⓛ 11.30–02.00

Pri Miro £££ ❻ Either a fairly long walk from the centre of town or a short taxi ride is justified in order to experience this authentic Serbian restaurant. Bulgarians and Serbs share a love of grilled meats, and this is the place to taste the differences in style and taste. The firm favourites are the *pleskavice* (sausage-like patties of minced meat) and *cevapcici* (rissoles), and there are some very tasty relishes to go with either. One of Sofia's best restaurants. ⓐ Murphy Street 34 ⓣ (02) 943 7127 ⓛ 12.00–24.00

Seasons £££ ❼ Seasons has the best themed buffets in the city and Mondays, devoted to Bulgarian cuisine, provide an excellent introduction to the country's food. There is also an à la carte menu and, in the summer, tables on the terrace with views of Mount

ⓞ *The Soviet Army Monument*

Vitosha. ❸ Hilton Hotel, Bulgaria Boulevard 1 ❶ (02) 933 5050
🕒 06.30–23.30

Nightlife

Bar Na Kraia Na Vselenata In English this is named the Bar at the
End of the Universe and describes itself as themed around 'the
fragmented remains of an eventually ruined planet, which is
enclosed in a vast time bubble and projected forward in time to the
precise moment of The End of The Universe'. What you actually get
is a large circular bar and brightly painted walls, plus a lively scene
with a friendly atmosphere and a long list of cocktails. ❸ Studentski
Grad, Block 34, next to Entrance B ❶ (02) 962 5541
Ⓦ www.vselenata.com 🕒 09.00–02.00

Funky's Music Hall The neon sign behind the NDK helps locate this
bar, and it is worth looking into after seeing a movie because the
live music is occasionally worth staying for. ❸ Bulgaria Square 1,
National Palace of Culture ❶ (02) 916 6410 🕒 21.00–02.00

Marseille A café-club with a good reputation for party nights,
especially at weekends, playing retro, latino, pop and rock. ❸ Prof. Dr
Ivan Stranski Street 5, between Blocks 55 and 56, Studentski Grad
❶ (02) 968 1977 🕒 08.00–02.00

O! Shipka £ The main venue for live indie and alternative music,
with a constantly changing programme of acts; check out the
website. ❸ Shipka Street 11 ❶ (02) 944 9388
Ⓦ www.club-oshipka.com 🕒 18.00–02.00

🔘 *The stunningly beautiful Rila Monastery*

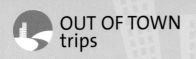

Mount Vitosha

Mount Vitosha is clearly visible from the city centre, and it only takes a 7-km (4⅓-mile) bus ride to reach the foothills of this 2,290-m high (7,513-ft) outcrop of rock and pine forests. There are a number of marked trails through the woods and, outside of winter, a day out with a picnic suggests itself as an ideal excursion from the city. You can take a bus to either Dragalevtsi and walk to a chair-lift to Aleko

PUBLIC TRANSPORT TO MOUNT VITOSHA

Hladilnika bus station, the one used to reach Boyana (see page 106), serves the Mount Vitosha area and to reach the station take tram No 9 on Alabin Street a five-minute walk away from Sveta Nedelya Square. The tram terminates at Hladilnika and after getting off the tram walk for half a minute through the small market of wooden stalls beside the tram lines. This brings you out onto a main street where you turn left and walk past a number of bus stops to a large open area where buses turn and where there is a ticket kiosk on your left and more bus stops. From here, bus No 64 goes to Dragalevtsi village; No 93 goes through the village and on to the chair-lift; No 98 goes to Dragalevtsi and onto Simeonovo village; and No 122 goes to the Simeonovo cable-car. You can use your usual tram tickets on these routes.

Bus No 66 goes to Aleko but for this route you need to purchase a separate return ticket from the kiosk. The times of the return buses are posted on the window of the kiosk and it is worth taking note of these. There are currently eight a day; the first departure at 07.50 and the last return bus at 18.00.

Mount Vitosha

from the village square, or to Simeonovo for a cable-car to Aleko.
A bus also goes directly to Aleko, and this would be your route if
planning a skiing trip in winter.

SIGHTS & ATTRACTIONS

Aleko

Aleko styles itself as a winter resort, and it is the base for skiing but,
skiing apart, the visitor infrastructure is decrepit and the sight of a
disused hotel sinking into the snow is hardly inspiring. There is a
functioning hotel with a restaurant at the point where the bus from
Sofia terminates, and that is about it. From the hotel, it is a five-
minute walk to the ski slopes. In summer, it takes less than an hour
for an invigorating walk up to Cherni Vruh (Black Peak), the summit
of Mount Vitosha.

Dragalevtsi

If you want to get off the bus at Dragalevtsi village, look for a
lemon-painted building on the left side of the street and the

SKIING ON MOUNT VITOSHA

Skiing lasts from late December through to early April,
although the start and end times tend to vary from one year
to the next. Aleko is the base, and this is where Ski School
Aleko (☎ (02) 967 1141) is based. Skiing gear can be hired by
the day and the current rate is 25lv a day. English-speaking
instructors can be hired, subject to 24 hours notice, at 25lv an
hour but a discount brings this down to 20lv if more than one
hour is booked.

cobbled Tsar Ivan Alexander Square. The journey from Hladilnika bus station only takes about seven minutes. There are hotels with restaurants in Dragalevtsi, and from here it takes about 40 minutes to walk up to the chair-lift. Facing the square from the bus stop, take the road that begins in the top right corner of the square and after about half an hour turn left off the road where a sign points to the

⏶ *Snow-capped Mount Vitosha*

Vodenitzata restaurant. The chair-lift is less than ten minutes away up this road, behind the Russian spa, and it stops at a mid-way station on its way up to Aleko.

ⓘ Chair-lift: (02) 967 1125 ⓒ 08.30–16.30 Fri–Sun. 1.5lv each way

Simeonovo

The village of Simeonovo is less attractive than Dragalevtsi (which itself is not especially eye-catching) and, with fewer amenities by way of places to eat, the only reason to come here would be to take the cable-car up to Aleko.

ⓘ Cable-car: (02) 961 2189 ⓒ 08.30–16.30 Tues–Sat, closed Mon

Zlatni Mostove

Zlatni Mostove (Golden Bridges) is an attractive area of evergreen forest and the misleadingly named Stone River, which is not really a river but a dramatic series of huge boulders deposited at the end of the last ice age under which flows a paltry stream. From where the Sofia bus stops, there is a number of marked hiking routes and, if you are making a day of it, take the one to Cherni Vruh, the peak of Mount Vitosha. It takes almost three hours, so be sure to bring water and food because there are no restaurants along the way. What you do get is a mildly spectacular landscape of peat bog.

Ⓝ Bus: No 61 from Ovcha Kupel bus station in Sofia (see 'Public Transport to Rila Monastery' on how to get to Ovcha Kupel). You will need to purchase a separate ticket for this route at the bus station.

▶ *The Stone River at Zlatni Mostove*

TAKING A BREAK

Hotel Restaurant Moreni £ On your left where the bus from Sofia terminates, this is the main restaurant at Aleko. The formal dining area is downstairs but you can order food from the menu and eat it in the bar area where large glass windows overlook the rustic scenery and where, in winter, a comforting log fire keeps the place warm. The food is the usual mix of grills, omelettes, mackerel and trout. ⓐ Aleko, Mount Vitosha ⓒ (02) 967 1059 ⓒ 08.00–24.00

Chili Pepper £–££ The menu features a full range of salads and other cold dishes like smoked salmon or shrimp cocktail, and many lunchtime meals such as chicken bites with bacon, aubergine pastry and meat rolls. Pork, chicken and fish meals also available. To find the restaurant, keep the village square on your left and walk 200 m (219 yds) further along Krairechna Street, the road where the bus from Sofia stops, and it is on your right. ⓐ Krairechna Street 26, Dragalevtsi ⓣ (02) 967 2220 ⓒ 11.00–22.00

The Old House £–££ This is one of the most pleasant places to enjoy a meal in Dragalevtsi, and you will find it by taking the road that leads from the village square to the chair-lift. It is on the left, less than five minutes from the village and, although the name is not in English, is easy to identify by its rustic-looking, alpine exterior. ⓐ General Kovatchev Street 9 ⓣ (02) 967 3137 ⓒ 12.00–24.00

AFTER DARK

Hotel Darling Restaurant ££ Black caviar for starters, specialities like *boyar shashik*, fried trout and a host of chicken, veal and pork dishes help to make this restaurant well worth considering for an evening meal. ❸ Yabalkova Gradina Street ❶ (02) 967 5018

Vodenitzata ££–£££ A folksy-looking, stone-built restaurant with an attractive garden area. The food is traditional Bulgarian, and evenings are enlivened by troupes of dancers in folk costumes. It is best to make a reservation at weekends because large groups can take over the place. ❸ By the Dragalevtsi chair-lift, Dragalevtsi ❶ (02) 967 1058 ❹ 12.00–24.00

ACCOMMODATION

Alexander Palace £ Close to the village square, this is the best hotel in Dragalevtsi in terms of amenities and general comfort. Standard rooms have a fridge and there is little to be gained by paying extra for one of the deluxe doubles. There is a restaurant and sauna. ❸ Nartzis Street 1, Dragalevtsi ❶ (02) 967 1184 ❶ (02) 967 3146 ❿ www.svetasofia-alexanders.com

Darling £ The second-best hotel in Dragalevtsi, with room rates a little less than those of the Alexander Palace but with a better restaurant (see page 124). ❸ Yabalkova Gradina Street 14, Dragalevtsi ❶ (02) 967 5018 ❺ hotel_darling@abv.bg and hotel_darling@yahoo.com

Edi £ There are 14 inexpensive double rooms in this small but basically comfortable hotel, and a restaurant on the first floor as well as outdoor tables for food and drink. The Chili Pepper restaurant (see page 124) is next door. ❸ Krairechna Street 28, Dragalevtsi ❶ (02) 967 2270 ❶ (02) 967 2218 ❺ hoteledi@bgnet.bg

Blagoevgrad

Two hours away by a regular bus service and 100 km (62 miles) south of Sofia, the university town of Blagoevgrad offers a day out to an animated and sophisticated city filled with bars, restaurants and a modicum of cultural attractions. Buses leave from Sofia's Central Bus Station, up to ten a day and with most leaving in the morning (last departure is 15.30), and stop either in front of Blagoevgrad's railway station or at the bus terminal 200 m (219 yds) further along the road. If you are dropped off at the bus terminal, walk out on to the street, turn left and walk the 200 m (219 yds) to the railway station and the junction. Turn right at the junction and walk up Brata Miladinovi, past the Alenmak hotel to the main and clearly identified American University of Bulgaria. If you go to the right in front of the main building and cut through the small park, this will bring you into town and straight to the pavement tables outside the Pizza Napoli restaurant. The centre of town is mostly pedestrianised, and the old part of town, Varosha, is on the other side of the small river and only a short walk away.

SIGHTS & ATTRACTIONS

Varosha

Varosha is the old quarter of the city, easy to reach on the other side of the river and readily identified by the cobbled streets and the traditional buildings that date back to the 19th century. Here you will find the Church of the Annunciation of the Virgin, its exterior characterised by red and white stripes and murals decorating the portico. The folksy-looking Kristo Hotel is directly above the church.

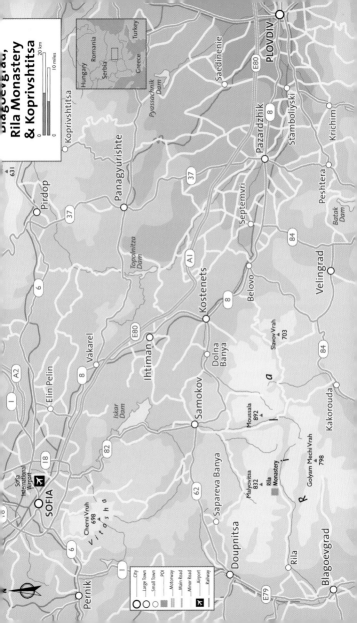

CULTURE

History Museum

A motley collection of assorted finds from ancient times, religious artefacts in the form of icons and carvings, and outbursts of colour in a fine display of traditional costumes from the region. There is also a natural history section made up of stuffed birds and animals. None of the labelling is in English, but the cost of admission includes a brochure in English.

ⓐ Alexander Stamboliysky Boulevard ⓣ (073) 823 557 ⓛ 09.00–12.00, 13.00–18.00 Mon–Sat, closed Sun. Admission charge

RETAIL THERAPY

Mason Fairly typical of the small boutiques catering to the city's students and young people – cotton fabrics, funky, loose-fitting garments for both sexes – Mason is on the same street as Tuborg (see page 132). ⓐ Bratia Kitanovi 10, Blagoevgrad ⓣ (073) 881 9752 ⓛ 11.00–19.30

RETAIL TRAUMA

For a shock-inducing glimpse of what shopping used to be like in the Soviet era, drop into the Rym department store. Its dark and gloomy interior, filled with displays so depressing that they act like an instant antidote to any consumerist urges, is left over from another age.

ⓐ Directly opposite the Kristal café in Macedonia Square

TAKING A BREAK

Kristal £ Dominating one corner of Macedonia Square, with its outdoor tables and always busy, this is the place to sink into with an hour to spare and watch the world, well Blagoevgrad, go by.
ⓐ Macedonia Square, Blagoevgrad ⓣ (073) 22876 ⓛ 08.30–24.00

Pizza Napoli £ If walking into town from the bus station, this is the first restaurant you will see, and its tasty food, good service and

△ *Vernacular architecture in Blagoevgrad*

commanding position between the university and the town centre makes it very popular at lunchtimes. There are plenty of outdoor tables, too, for relaxing with a drink – Bulgarian champagne is on the drinks list – before or after the busy hours. ⓐ Hristo Botev Square, Blagoevgrad ⓣ (073) 7788 ⓛ 08.30–24.00

Tuborg £ A spacious and comfortable pub-restaurant on one of the pedestrianised streets running off Macedonia Square. Salads, spaghetti and meat dishes, with tables outside. ⓐ Bratia Kitanovi 5, Blagoevgrad ⓣ (073) 881 2367 ⓛ 08.00–01.00

Varosha Restaurant £ Situated between the museum and the church in the old part of town, this timbered two-storey building blends in perfectly with the traditional ambiance of the neighbourhood. The menu is unexciting but adequate for a lunch break, and there are two tables on a neat little balcony overlooking the river and park where you could happily while away the time with a drink. ⓐ Komitrov Street, Blagoevgrad ⓣ (073) 881 370 ⓛ 09.00–23.00

AFTER DARK

Restaurants
Kristo £–££ On the first floor of the hotel and decked out in the traditional style that one would expect, this roomy restaurant has a menu that includes 40 different salads, hot and cold starters and grills. The décor of dark wood gives the restaurant a rather sober atmosphere, and the best tables are those overlooking the cobbled courtyard. ⓐ Kristo Hotel, Komitrov Street, Varosha, Blagoevgrad ⓣ (073) 880 444

Dream ££ Around the corner from Pizza Napoli and upstairs from the Underground pub, this is the most formal restaurant in the city in the evening. The menu is not in English but staff should be able to translate; stick with the fish dishes because this is what they do best. **ⓐ** Arseni Kostentzev Street 7, Blagoevgrad **ⓘ** 0899 940761 **ⓛ** 09.00–01.00

Nightlife

Underground This is the most popular nightspot in Blagoevgrad, and the place is packed with students for the weekend discos. There is also a separate bar but it is hard to escape the sound system blasting out rock and pop-folk. **ⓐ** Arseni Kostentzev Street 7, Blagoevgrad **ⓘ** 0897 829488 **ⓛ** 20.00–02.00

Vertigo No food but a long drinks list and lots of cocktails. **ⓐ** Todor Alexandrov Street 3, Blagoevgrad **ⓘ** 0899 786322 **ⓛ** 24 hours

ACCOMMODATION

Kristo £ This would be the first choice for any overnight stay in Blagoevgrad. It is situated in the peaceful Varosha district but within walking distance of the city's nightlife. There are over 30 rooms with air-conditioning, a restaurant and bar, and a sauna. **ⓐ** Komitrov Street, Varosha, Blagoevgrad **ⓘ** (073) 880 444 **ⓕ** (073) 880 555 **ⓔ** hotel_kristo@abv.bg

Rila Monastery

The Rila Mountains lie to the south of Mount Vitosha, but it takes longer to reach the famed Rila Monastery, 120 km (75 miles) from Sofia. Although a day trip from the capital is feasible, most visitors spend a night outside Sofia in order to make the journey a less hectic one.

SIGHTS & ATTRACTIONS

Rila Mountains

Quite apart from the attractions of the monastery itself, hiking the rural trails through the surrounding forests is reason enough to make an excursion to this famous valley in the Rila Mountains. A number of trails start from near the monastery and the shortest, less than an hour's walk, leads to St John of Rila's cave. This route begins 2 km (1¹/₄ miles) east of the monastery's eastern gate (the main entrance to

PUBLIC TRANSPORT TO RILA MONASTERY

The Ovcha Kupel bus station (☏ (02) 955 5362), on Ovcha Kupel Boulevard, which is off Tsar Boris III Boulevard and southwest of the city centre, serves Rila Monastery. To reach the bus station, take tram No 5 from Alabin Street and, after about ten stops, you will see it on the right side of the street. Confirm the time of the first bus running direct to the monastery, and the last buses back, and catch the first bus if making a day trip from Sofia. A more leisurely itinerary would be to catch one of the numerous daily buses from Ovcha Kupel to Dupnitsa, and from there catch a local bus to the monastery, spending a night close to the monastery at Rilets Hotel or in the monastery itself.

the monastery is through the western gate) by taking the trail that heads left just after the Bachhkova Cheshna restaurant. When you reach the cave, you can walk through it and come out the other side but it is unlighted and very claustrophobic.

The main trails through the Rila Mountains are set out on a noticeboard in the monastery's car park, and a bracing walk can be enjoyed by taking any one of them. ⓐ Rila Monastery is 27 km (16³/₄ miles) east of Rila village on a signposted road that branches off the E79, 20 km (12¹/₂ miles) south of Dupnitsa

CULTURE

Rila Monastery

Coming from Sofia, you arrive outside the fortress-like western gate and pass through it into a serene courtyard surrounded by stylish striped arcades, tiers of monastic chambers and graceful balconies. Climb the staircase to the top balcony to take in the scenery. The

THE HISTORY OF THE MONASTERY

The monastery owes its origins to Ivan Rilski, now known as St John of Rila, a 9th-century hermit monk who acquired a band of devotees after lengthy sojourns in the wild, and eventually founded a hermitage in the Rila Mountains. The first monastery, a short distance from the original hermitage, was founded in 1335 and became a major spiritual centre during the Middle Ages. It survived for half a millennium until it was accidentally burned down in the 19th century; rebuilding started within a year and what you see today was added to UNESCO's list of World Heritage Sites in the early 1980s.

monastery's kitchen, in the west wing to the left of the church that occupies the centre of the courtyard, is well worth a visit.

The church museum is to be found in the east wing. Its claim to fame is a late 18th-century wooden cross, intricately inscribed with 140 biblical scenes and 1,500 human figures, the work of one monk who devoted 12 years of his life to the task and lost his eyesight as a consequence of spending hours squinting through a magnifying glass.

ⓐ Rila Monastery, 27 km (16¾ miles) east of Rila village, off the E79, 20 km (12½ miles) south of Dupnitsa ⓒ 06.00–22.00 (summer); 08.00–18.00 (winter); Museum: 08.00–17.00. Free admission to monastery; admission charge for museum

Rila Monastery Church

Built in the 1830s and the largest monastery church in the country, the exterior is covered in murals and the interior walls are adorned with frescoes, all of which invite close scrutiny for their pictorial spectacles and wealth of detail.

ⓒ 06.00–22.00 (summer); 08.00–18.00 (winter)

TAKING A BREAK

Rila Monastery Bakery £ A monkish repast of *mekitsi* (deep-fried doughnuts), bread and sheep yogurt. ⓐ Outside the east gate of Rila Monastery ⓒ 06.00–22.00 (summer); 08.00–18.00 (winter)

Restaurant Drushliavitsa £–££ This is easily the most attractive place for a meal when visiting Rila Monastery: a scenic location with outdoor tables taking advantage of the views and a full menu of Bulgarian dishes and fresh trout. ⓐ Outside the east gate of Rila Monastery ⓣ (07054) 278 756 ⓒ 08.00–22.00

ACCOMMODATION

Rila Monastery £ Spartan accommodation in monks' cells is available at the monastery but you will have to do without hot water. Check what time the monastery gates close and plan accordingly for dinner. ⓐ Rila Monastery ⓣ (07054) 2208

Rilets £ A 15-minute walk from the eastern gate of Rila Monastery brings you to this featureless but functional hotel. It would do for a one-night stopover and there is a restaurant, although it would be better to eat at Restaurant Drushliavitsa (see page 124) and get back to the hotel before dark. ⓐ Rila Monastery ⓣ (07054) 2106

◆ You can stay overnight at Rila Monastery

Koprivshtitsa

Koprivshtitsa, a small town 75 km (46½ miles) east of Sofia, is noted for its traditional Balkan architecture. The town also played a key role in an insurrection against Ottoman rule in 1876, called the April Uprising. It takes about two hours to reach Koprivshtitsa from Sofia by public transport, using one of the two minibuses that depart daily in the morning from the Trafik-Market bus terminal next to the Central Railway Station. The bus stop in Koprivshtitsa is in the middle of town and it is a short walk northwards, following the river, to reach the main 20 April Square. In the northwest corner of the square, at No 6, there is a tourist information centre (☎ 07184 2191 ⏰ erratic but officially 09.00–18.00). Two doors up is the Kupchiinitsa (museums' office) (⏰ 09.00–17.00), and here you can purchase a combined ticket for the town's six museum houses; this saves money if you visit more than two of them but otherwise pay individually at each museum. Try to avoid visiting the town on a Monday, when many of the house museums are closed. The best museum house to see from the outside is Oslekov House; the best interior is Lyutov House.

SIGHTS & ATTRACTIONS

Oslekov House

This house was built in the middle of the 19th century for a rich merchant family, and the façade is painted with cityscapes of Rome, Venice and Padua – places visited by the merchant. A timber staircase leads to a hall, and a set of rooms laid out with exhibits relating to the history of the house and the lifestyle of its

● *Mother of local poet Dimcho Debelyanov waits for him to return from WWI*

inhabitants. The house is a couple of minutes away on foot and uphill from 20 April Square.

📍 Garanilo Street 📞 (01784) 2555 🕐 09.30–17.00 Tues–Sun, 09.30–12.00 Mon. Admission charge

Dimcho Debelyanov House

From Oslekov House, continue uphill and turn the corner into Dimcho Debelyanov Street to find this house on the left-hand side after 100 m (110 yds). Birthplace of the poet Dimcho Debelyanov (1887–1916), the exhibits on display relate to his tragic life but the captions are woefully inadequate. Debelyanov was killed in World War I, and his love life was marred by the early death of a woman whose father killed her to prevent her relationship with Debelyanov continuing.

📍 Dimcho Debelyanov Street 6 📞 (01784) 2077 🕐 09.30–17.00 Tues–Sun, closed Mon. Admission charge

Todor Kabeshkov House

From Dimcho Debelyanov House, return to Garanilo Street and turn right to reach the top of the hill and the town cemetery. Over the grave of the poet stands a statue, and the small church is also worth a visit. If you turn left after leaving the churchyard on the side opposite to where you came in, you will find Todor Kabeshkov House some 40 m (44 yds) down the street on your left. The curvy lines of each side of the house's façade are a characteristic feature of the vernacular architecture. The interior is devoted to displays of material relating to the April Uprising, the house being the birthplace of the hero who began the insurrection.

📍 Todor Kabeshkov Street 8 📞 (01784) 2054 🕐 09.30–17.30 Tues–Sun, closed Mon. Admission charge

Lyutov House

Cross the bridge after leaving Todor Kabeshkov Street and turn left into Nikola Belovezhdov Street to find the white-painted Lyutov House on your left after 100 m (110 yds). The home of a rich and much-travelled merchant, the interior is richly decorated with murals of European locations visited by the merchant, ornately carved ceilings and Viennese furniture.

ⓐ Nikola Belovezhdov Street 2 ❶ (01784) 2138 ⏰ 09.30–17.00 Tues–Sun, closed Mon. Admission charge

🔺 *Overlooking the town*

TAKING A BREAK

Bulgaria £ This restaurant has a lovely terrace as well as tables in a comfortable dining area that evokes times past. It is situated on the main street that runs by the side of the river and links the bus stop with April 20 Square, but at its northern end and beyond the main square. ⓐ Hadzhi Nencho Palaveev Boulevard 31 ⓣ (01784) 2183 ⓛ 09.00–22.30

Chuchura £ Easy to find, close by the bus stop, this inexpensive eatery is very convenient if you arrive in town feeling hungry and thirsty after the journey from Sofia. Do not be put off by the unprepossessing exterior, the food is good and relies on traditional Bulgarian favourites. ⓐ Hadzhi Nencho Palaveev Boulevard 66 ⓣ (01784) 2712 ⓛ 09.00–22.30

Pod Staata Krusha £ This pub-restaurant is cheap and cheerful and offers a good range of drinks and meals throughout the day and evening. ⓐ Hadzhi Nencho Palaveev Boulevard 56 ⓣ (01784) 2163 ⓛ 08.30–22.30

AFTER DARK

Restaurant
Dyado Liben £ This restaurant, on the eastern side of the river and reached by a bridge from the town square, is set in a picturesque old house with an attractive cobbled courtyard and inside seating upstairs. The food is not particularly different to what is found on

● *Glorious countryside around Koprivshtitsa*

other restaurant menus in Koprivshtitsa, but the old building and furnishings lend an atmosphere ideally suited for an evening out.
ⓐ Hadzhi Nencho Palaveev Boulevard 47 ⓣ (01784) 2109
ⓛ 09.00–22.00

ACCOMMODATION

Accommodation can be booked at the tourist information office but there should be no problem finding a place to stay. Hotels, usually small family-run affairs, are dotted around town and room rates are fairly uniform and very affordable.

Astra £ At the northeast corner of the village, 0.5 km (⅓ mile) from the town square and on the other side of the river, this family-run guesthouse has comfortable rooms in a traditional setting and benefits from a pretty courtyard where you can sit with a beer or two and see the evening out. ⓐ Hadzhi Nencho Palaveev Boulevard 11 ⓣ (01784) 2364 ⓦ www.hotelastra.org

Bashtina Kushta £ If you want a break from the folksy style that characterises most places in town, this modern hostelry fits the bill. Uncomplicated rooms and attic ones with sloping ceilings. Walk north from the town square and it is on your left after 150 m (164 yds). ⓐ Hadzhi Nencho Palaveev Boulevard 32 ⓣ (01784) 3033 ⓦ www.fhhotel.info

---

ⓞ *It helps if you can decipher some of the Cyrillic letters*

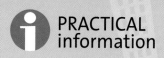

Directory

GETTING THERE

You are most likely to arrive in Sofia by air, with direct flights from the UK and indirect flights from Ireland, North America, Australia and New Zealand. Arriving by car will take forever and cost a lot in petrol, while taking a train is only likely to make sense if you are travelling with a rail pass and Bulgaria is one more country on your itinerary.

By air from the UK and Ireland

British Airways and Bulgaria Air fly direct from London (3 hours and 20 minutes) but their fares are expensive. Wizzair flies direct from Luton with reasonable fares. Indirect fares via other European cities, and with other airlines, currently offer the best fare deals. Malev Hungarian Airlines, for example, flies to Sofia via Budapest from the UK and Ireland. Also, check out specialist agents like Balkan Holidays and compare their prices.

Balkan Holidays ✆ 0845 130 1114 ⓦ www.balkanholidays.co.uk
British Airways ✆ 0845 773 3377 ⓦ www.britishairways.com
Bulgaria Air ✆ 020 7637 7637 ⓦ www.balkanair.co.uk
Malev ✆ 020 7439 0577 ⓦ www.malev.hu
Regent Holidays ✆ 0117 921 1711 ⓦ www.regent-holidays.co.uk
Wizzair ⓦ www.wizzair.com

Many people are aware that air travel emits CO_2, which contributes to climate change. You may be interested in the possibility of lessening the environmental impact of your flight through the charity Climate Care, which offsets your CO_2 by funding environmental projects around the world. Visit www.climatecare.org

By rail from the UK and Ireland

There are various rail routes but, at the moment, it is still not possible to buy a through train ticket to Sofia. The closest you can get is a booked ticket to Budapest and, once there, no problem should arise booking a ticket for the daily Budapest–Sofia train service. It will take about 24 hours to reach Budapest from London (Eurostar to Paris and on from there by sleeper via Vienna or Munich), and the last leg of the journey, Budapest–Sofia, will take that long again.

The Man in Seat 61 Ⓦ www.seat61.com

Rail Europe Ⓦ www.raileurope.co.uk (UK)
www.eurorailways.com (US)

Thomas Cook European Rail Timetable ℡ 01733 416477 (UK) 1800 322 3834 (US) Ⓦ www.thomascookpublishing.com

Traineurope UK ℡ 0900 195 0101 Ⓦ www.traineurope.co.uk

ENTRY FORMALITIES

Visa requirements

No visa is required by citizens of the UK, Ireland, the US, Australia, New Zealand and Canada for a single visit of 30 days. Other EU citizens can visit without a visa for 90 days. Officially, visitors are still required to register as a foreigner, but if you are staying in a hotel or hostel this piece of bureaucracy should be done for you and you may be given a completed registration form to keep in your passport. In theory, you could be fined for not having the form when you depart, but in practice no attention is paid to this for short-stay foreigners from Western countries.

Customs

You are not allowed to export antiques or art works without a permit issued by the Ministry of Culture, and this should be arranged by the shop concerned. Import limits for EU and non-EU travellers include 1 litre of spirits or wine and 200 cigarettes.

MONEY

The Bulgarian currency is the lev, plural leva (lv), divided into 100 stotinki. The denominations for notes are 1, 2, 5, 10, 20, 50, 100 and 200; there are coins in denominations of 1 and 2 leva, and coins for 1, 2, 5, 10, 20 and 50 stotinki. The euro is sometimes accepted (including taxi drivers from the airport) because the lev is pegged to the European currency and there are no wild fluctuations.

It is not easy to obtain Bulgarian currency outside of the country, but there is no need to do so as ATMs are to be found at the airport and outside banks throughout the city. There are limits on how much can be withdrawn on any one day, and for this reason alone it makes sense to bring some cash in your home currency with you. It helps to have more than one bank debit card and/or, as a backup, some Thomas Cook or American Express traveller's cheques in sterling, US dollars or euros. Money can be exchanged at banks (🕓 09.00–16.00 Mon–Fri), and private exchange bureaux are also dotted around the city centre, although rates vary and should be checked (the ones on Vitosha Boulevard are best avoided). You will find it difficult to exchange any Bulgarian leva once you return home so plan accordingly. Credit cards are widely accepted in shops and restaurants.

In the Communist era there used to be a black market for the Bulgarian currency, and you may still find yourself approached by someone claiming to offer an exchange rate way above the official one. This will almost certainly be a scam and, through sleight of hand, you will find yourself with a wad of paper topped with one genuine banknote.

HEALTH, SAFETY & CRIME

There are no compulsory vaccinations. Tap water is chlorinated and safe for brushing teeth, but for drinking it is best to use the bottled water that is available everywhere in the city. Should you suffer from a mild stomach complaint or diarrhoea, pharmacies (**аптека**) sell standard treatments and oral rehydration salts. Pharmacies may have English-speaking staff, but don't rely on this – if you require attention and prescription drugs head for a private medical clinic or hospital. See the 'Emergencies' section (page 156) for contact details.

Sofia is safer than most major European cities, but common sense dictates safety precautions with regard to personal possessions and safety. Pickpockets operate in crowded places in the city centre.

Keep a list of the numbers of your traveller's cheques with your proof of purchase (which will be needed for a claim), and the contact number to use in case the cheques are lost or stolen. Store this information separately from the cheques themselves; posting them to an email account is a good idea. Retain a photocopy of the main page of your passport and keep this separate from your passport. Consider storing the number of your passport, or a

HEALTH INFORMATION

Websites for health and travel advice from the British government

Ⓦ www.doh.gov.uk/travellers and www.fco.gov.uk/travel

Useful tips and information. Ⓦ www.travelhealth.co.uk

Travel Health Online Ⓦ www.tripprep.com

Websites for American travellers

Ⓦ www.cdc.gov/travel and www.healthfinder.com

World Health Organization Ⓦ www.who.int/en

scanned copy of the relevant pages, in an email that can be retrieved if necessary. See 'Emergencies' (page 156) for contact telephone numbers.

OPENING HOURS

Opening hours of museums and attractions are usually 10.00–18.00 and some close on Mondays. Government office hours are 08.00–12.00 and 13.30–17.00, Mon–Sat. Bank hours are 09.00–16.00. General shopping hours are 08.30–18.00, Mon–Sat, but many stay open until 19.00 or 20.00. Markets open from around 08.30 to around 18.30. The small kiosks, which are a characteristic feature of the city, sell drinks, snacks, phone cards and a variety of other items, and tend to stay open until 21.00 or 22.00.

TOILETS

Public toilets, especially clean ones, are not common in Sofia, although you can find decent ones at Halite (see page 72), the underpass at NDK (see page 90), and in the Tzum shopping mall (see page 71). Hotels and good restaurants can always be used if necessary.

TRAVEL INSURANCE

It is highly advisable to arrange travel insurance before travelling to Sofia because there are no reciprocal health schemes with EU countries. A good policy will cover medical treatment, baggage cover and theft or loss of possessions. You will need to make a police report for non-medical claims, and ensure that you keep any receipts for medical treatment. Consider keeping a copy of your policy and emergency contact numbers in your email account.

CHILDREN

There are not many sights or attractions that are obviously suited to children, and time spent in old churches and museums is likely to bore them. The parks offer open space, and there is a play area in Borisova Gradina (see page 104). A trip to Mount Vitosha should prove engaging for energetic children and, if new to skiing, they could be introduced to the sport at Aleko. Trips on the chair-lift and cable-car will be fun, although with young children beware of the fact that the safety bar at the Dragalevtsi chair-lift needs to be manually set by the rider. Cinema screenings are worth checking for suitable movies, and the Galaxy Bowling alley (see page 34) offers fun for all the family.

🔺 A typical street kiosk

Sofia is generally a child-friendly place, and there are no problems with hotels and restaurants. For baby food and disposable nappies, use the Bonjour supermarket in Lege Street or the one in the Tzum shopping mall (see page 71). Finding suitable food should not be difficult and, although children's menus are rare, there will usually be suitable dishes, and familiar Western fast-food franchises can be found in the city. At the Sunday brunch at Flannagans (see page 85) a children's buffet is provided and there is a supervised children's area with video screenings. Children are defined as being under 12 years of age.

- **Sofia Land** An amusement park, to the east of Yuzhen Park and a short taxi ride away from the city centre, with plenty to do on a family outing. Rides on a giant wheel, jumping nets, carousel, inflatable galleon, mini scooters. ⓐ Nikola Vaptzarov Boulevard ⓣ (02) 269 1111 ⓦ www.sofialand.bg ⓛ 11.00–19.00. Main castle area: admission free. Various rides: individual charges

COMMUNICATIONS
Phones
There are three types of pay phones in the city. The coin-operated ones that use 0.50lv tokens, which can be purchased from most kiosks you see dotted around the city, are suitable only for local calls. This type of phone booth is being phased out, and even the ones you do find may turn out to be broken. More common and far easier to use are the two card-operated types of public phones: the blue Mobikon and the orange Bulfon types. Each uses its own phone cards, which can be purchased from kiosks and used for long-distance calls. As is usually the case with

hotels, telephone rates for calls made from your bedroom have a significant mark-up, and it is more economical to use a phone card.

Mobiles

Mobile reception is good, and you should be able to make and receive calls and texts on your mobile phone. Check with your home network before departure about the cost of making and receiving such calls and text messages; they can be exorbitantly high.

Internet

Internet access is available in the city through internet cafés like the excellent Site Internet Café (see page 102). Most hotels provide access to the internet for guests, and while most will charge for this, others offer it as a free service. Hotel staff should also be able to guide you to the nearest internet café. The main post office (see below) also provides internet access. Wireless internet is spreading quickly and operates in some hotels – the Radisson SAS (see page 41), for example, is completely wireless – as well as some cafés (such as the Onda, see page 84).

Post offices

The Central Post Office is at Gurko Street 6 (see the Sveta Nedelya map, page 63) (ⓘ (02) 980 1225 ⓒ 07.00–20.30 Mon–Sat,

> ### TELEPHONING BULGARIA
> The international country code for telephoning Bulgaria is 359 and this is followed by the Sofia city code, which is 2, followed by the seven-digit number you are telephoning.

TELEPHONING ABROAD

Dial 00, which is the international access code, followed by your country code and then the area code minus the initial zero, followed by the number itself.

Country codes

Australia: 61
Canada: 1
France: 33
Germany: 49
Ireland: 353
New Zealand: 64
South Africa: 27
UK: 44
USA: 1

08.00–13.00 Sun). International calls can be made from metered phones and paid to a cashier. Internet access is also available. Planetphone (@ Stefan Karadza Street 18B, parallel to Gurko Street on the block to the south ○ 10.00–22.00 Mon–Sat, 12.00–22.00 Sun) offers cheap international calls.

Postcards and letters to Europe cost 1lv, to North America 1.40lv.

TELEPHONING IN BULGARIA

For local calls in Sofia just dial the seven-digit number.
Directory inquiries: 124
International operator: 0123

◀ *The Radisson SAS*

ELECTRICITY

The electricity rate is the normal European one of 220V, 50Hz, which means that European appliances will work without a problem. Plugs come in the form of two round prongs so you may need an adaptor. American appliances using 110–120 volts will need an adaptor and a transformer. Mid-range and more expensive hotels will have 110-volt shaver outlets. See Ⓦ www.kropla.com for more information.

TRAVELLERS WITH DISABILITIES

Sofia is not geared up for travellers with disabilities. Most museums and other places of interest, including churches, are not well equipped for visitors in wheelchairs. Streets and pavements can be cracked and uneven, and are rarely sloped for wheelchair use. Toilets for the disabled are rare, and public transport can present a challenge. Before booking your flight, check with some airlines about the facilities they can offer at Sofia International Airport. A guide to international airlines and the facilities and services they provide for passengers with disabilities can be found at Ⓦ www.allgohere.com

FURTHER INFORMATION

There is no tourist information office in Sofia and you will find yourself relying on staff at your hotel or hostel for most enquiries.

Tourist websites

Websites with information, listings and maps:

Ⓦ www.bulgaria.com
Ⓦ www.sofia.com
Ⓦ www.sofiacityguide.com
Ⓦ www.programata.bg

Ⓦ www.hotels-in-bulgaria.com
Ⓦ www.sofiaecho.com

BACKGROUND READING

A Concise History of Bulgaria, R J Crampton
The Balkan Cookbook: Traditional Cooking from Romania, Bulgaria and the Balkan Countries, Trish Davies, Lesley Chamberlain

🔺 Ask your hotel staff if you need help with transportation

Useful phrases

Although English is spoken in Bulgaria, these words and phrases may come in handy. See also the phrases for specific situations in other parts of this book.

English	Bulgarian	*Approx. pronunciation*
BASICS		
Yes	Да	*Dah*
No	Не	*Neh*
Please	Моля	*Molya*
Thank you	Благодаря	*Blagodarya*
Hello	Здравейте	*Zdraveiteh*
Goodbye	Довиждане	*Dovizhdaneh*
Excuse me	Извинете	*Izvinyavaite*
Sorry	Съжалявам	*Sazhalyavam*
That's OK	Няма проблеми	*Nyama problemi*
To	До	*Doh*
From	От	*Ot*
I don't speak Bulgarian	Не говоря български	*Ne govoryah bulgarski*
Do you speak English?	Говорите ли английски?	*Govoriteh li angleeski?*
Good morning	Добро утро	*Dobro utro*
Good afternoon	Добър ден	*Dobar den*
Good evening	Добър вечер	*Dobar vecher*
Good night	Лека нощ	*Lekah nosht*
My name is …	Казвам се …	*Kazvam se …*
DAYS & TIMES		
Monday	Понеделник	*Ponedelnik*
Tuesday	Вторник	*Vtornik*
Wednesday	Сряда	*Sryada*
Thursday	Четвъртък	*Chetvartak*
Friday	Петък	*Petak*
Saturday	Събота	*Sabotah*
Sunday	Неделя	*Nedelya*
Morning	Сутрин	*Sutrin*
Afternoon	Следобед	*Sledobed*
Evening	Вечер	*Vecher*
Night	Нощ	*Nosht*
Yesterday	Вчера	*Vchera*

English	Bulgarian	Approx. pronunciation
Today	Днес	Dnes
Tomorrow	Утре	Utreh
What time is it?	Колко е часът?	Kolko eh chasat?
It is …	Часът е …	Chasat eh …
09.00	Девет	Devet
Midday	Обед	Obed
Midnight	Полунощ	Polunosht

NUMBERS

One	Едно	Edno
Two	Две	Dveh
Three	Три	Trih
Four	Четири	Chetiri
Five	Пет	Pet
Six	Шест	Shess
Seven	Седем	Sedem
Eight	Осем	Osem
Nine	Девет	Devet
Ten	Десет	Desset
Eleven	Единайсет	Edinaiset
Twelve	Дванайсет	Dvanaiset
Twenty	Двайсет	Dvaiset
Fifty	Петдесет	Petdesset
One hundred	Сто	Stoh

MONEY

I would like to change these traveller's cheques/this currency	Искам да обменя тези пътнически чекове/тази валута	Iskam da obmenya tezi patnicheski checkoveh/tazi valuta
Where is the nearest ATM?	Къде се намира най-близкият банкомат?	Kudeh se namira nay blizkiyat bankomat?
Do you accept credit cards?	Приемате ли кредитни карти?	Priemate li kreditni karti?

SIGNS & NOTICES

Airport	Летище/Аерогара	Letishteh/Aerogara
Railway station	Ж. П. Гара	Zh. P. Gara
Platform	Перон	Peron
Smoking/ Non smoking	Пушенето забранено/ Пушенето позволено	Pusheneto zabraneno/ pusheneto pozvoleno
Toilets	Тоалетни	Toaletni
Ladies/Gentlemen	Жени/Мъже	Zheni/Muzheh
Underground	Метро	Metro

Emergencies

MEDICAL SERVICES

The **Accident and Emergency Hospital** for Sofia is the Pirogov Hospital (ⓐ Tsar Boris 3rd Boulevard, opposite the Rodina Hotel ⓣ (02) 915 411). Staff cannot be relied on to speak English. **Private medical clinics** include Gurgulyat Clinic (ⓐ Rakovski Street 148B ⓣ (02) 981 0331 ⓛ 08.00–20.00 Mon–Fri, 09.00–18.00 Sat, closed Sun) and the Vita Medical Centre (ⓐ Dragovitsa Street 9 ⓣ (02) 943 4398 ⓦ www.vita.bg ⓛ 24 hours).

⬥ *Police boxes are located at all major road junctions*

Dental clinics include Medstom Clinic (ⓐ Knyaz Dondukov Boulevard 26 ⓣ (02) 981 0000 ⓒ 24 hours) and Juniordent (ⓐ Patriarh Evtimil Boulevard 1 ⓣ (02) 988 3175).

24-hour pharmacies include Ana (ⓐ Vitosha Boulevard 95 ⓣ (02) 953 4157), Saldzhi (ⓐ Vitosha Boulevard 35 ⓣ (02) 980 5896) and Sofilski Apteki (ⓐ Sveta Nedelya Square 5 ⓣ (02) 987 5089).

Police ⓣ 160
Fire ⓣ 160
Ambulance ⓣ 150

EMBASSIES & CONSULATES

See ⓘ www.embassyworld.com for a full list of embassies and consulates.

Australia ⓐ Trakia Street 37 ⓣ (02) 946 1334
France ⓐ Oborishte Street 29 ⓣ (02) 965 1100
Germany ⓐ Juliot Curie Street 25 ⓣ (02) 918 380
Ireland ⓐ Bacho Kiro Street 26–30 ⓣ (02) 985 3425
UK ⓐ Moskovska Street 9 ⓣ (02) 933 9222
USA ⓐ Koziak Street 16 ⓣ (02) 937 5100

EMERGENCY PHRASES

Help! Помощ! *Pomosht!*   **Fire!** Пожар! *Pozhar!*
Stop! Стоп!/Спри! *Stop!/Spri!*

Call an ambulance/a doctor/the police/the fire brigade!
Извикайте линейка/лекар/полицията/пожарната!
Izvikaite lineika/lekar/politsiata/pozharnata!

INDEX

The publishers would like to thank the following for supplying their copyright photographs for this book: Alan Grant page 137; Zeynep Mufti pages 7, 13 & 49; Pictures Colour Library pages 1, 21, 29, 115, 127 & 139; Sheraton Sofia Hotel Balkan pages 41 & 73; Meeli Tamm pages 31, 33, 61, 141, 150, 153 & 156; Phil Wigglesworth pages 17, 95, 100, 103, 109, 113, 125 & 135; all the rest Sean Sheehan

Copy editor: Joanne Osborn
Proofreader: Lynn Bresler

Send your thoughts to
books@thomascook.com

- **Found a great bar, club, shop or must-see sight that we don't feature?**

- **Like to tip us off about any information that needs updating?**

- **Want to tell us what you love about this handy little guidebook and more importantly how we can make it even handier?**

Then here's your chance to tell all! Send us ideas, discoveries and recommendations today and then look out for your valuable input in the next edition of this title. As an extra 'thank you' from Thomas Cook Publishing, you'll be automatically entered into our exciting monthly prize draw.

Send an email to the above address (stating the book's title) or write to: CitySpots Project Editor, Thomas Cook Publishing, PO Box 227, The Thomas Cook Business Park, Unit 18, Coningsby Road, Peterborough PE3 8SB, UK.